THE 7 UNIVERSAL LAWS OF CUSTOMER VALUE

How to Win Customers & Influence Markets

THE 7 UNIVERSAL LAWS OF CUSTOMER VALUE

How to Win Customers & Influence Markets

STEPHEN C. BROYDRICK

This publication is designed to provide accurate and
authoritative information in regard to the subject matter
covered. It is sold with the understanding that neither the
author or the publisher is engaged in rendering legal, accounting,
or other professional service. If legal advice or other expert
assistance is required, the services of a competent professional
person should be sought.

From a Declaration of Principles jointly adopted by a Committee
of the American Bar Association and a Committee of Publishers.

◤◥ **Times Mirror**
◣◢ **Higher Education Group**

Library of Congress Cataloging-in-Publication Data

Broydrick, Stephen C.
    The 7 universal laws of customer value : how to win customers and influence
markets / by Stephen C. Broydrick.
        p. cm.
    Includes index.
    ISBN 0-7863-0732-3
    1. Customer services. 2. Consumer satisfaction. I. Title.
    HF5415.5.B76 1996
    658.8'12—dc20   96–12059
                                                                          C

Printed in the United States of America
1 2 3 4 5 6 7 8 9 0   3 2 1 0 9 8 7 6

CONTENTS

ACKNOWLEDGMENTS

This book was made possible by the contributions of both friends and colleagues. Cynthia Zigmund of Irwin Professional Publishing provided the initial encouragement when *The 7 Universal Laws* was just the kernel of an idea. Once writing began, I relied on the feedback of Robert Tucker and Stephen Schuit, who took the time to review the work at both the proposal and manuscript stage. Paula Broydrick provided careful editing and corrected my unpredictable grammar. She did so insistently but with good cheer. We still love each other.

And finally, I would like to thank those professionals who don't receive enough thanks—librarians. So much is being written about the wealth of information available on the Internet and on CD-ROMS, yet the best source of information remains your librarian. Every time I needed help with a source, a computer, or a microfilm or copy machine, the librarians at the Portland Public Library and the library of the University of Southern Maine were ready and willing to help. Thank you all for your dedicated service on this project.

INTRODUCTION

A recent television advertisement was created to drive dieters into delirium. It promotes the unique taste and convenience of Boboli® pizza shells. You feel like leaning into the screen to smell and savor the succulent, fresh ingredients as they're poured on the golden Boboli crust. Then, at the last possible moment, a graphic flashes across the screen: "New lower price." Twenty-eight seconds of deliciously adding value are wiped out by a two-second tag line about price. You wonder, "If this product is so good, why does it *need* a new lower price?"

A sales representative for United Parcel Service arrived at our office several months ago. He asked me who we're using for overnight shipping. "Federal Express," I told him. These two words created an instant declaration of war. He began a five minute dissertation on how much cheaper UPS® is than FedEx®. "We have lower rates in every conceivable category," he explained.

Not once did he discuss what made UPS *better* than FedEx. Is their service more reliable? He never said. Do they provide more accurate and timely tracking of packages? It wasn't mentioned. Are their customer service representatives courteous and experienced? Predicted response: "Of course. But have I told you yet that we're cheaper?"

Boboli's advertising and UPS's salesman had sent their products into a place I call *The Commodity Zone.* Think of The Commodity Zone as that spot in your customer's mind where all competing products and services look like plain vanilla pudding. The only way he can tell one pudding from the next is to look at the price tag. Customers aren't born with a Commodity Zone. Ill-conceived promotions that place the price ahead of features and benefits bring The Commodity Zone to life.

Once your product enters the Zone, escape is difficult. Just ask General Mills. In 1994, it cut back on costly coupons and grocery store promotions for its breakfast cereals. The Minnesota-based company was especially anxious to shed itself of buy-one-get-one-free promotions known in marketing circles as Bogos. As promotional deals were eliminated, General Mills executive Stephen W. Sanger chose to lower prices on many of his brands so that they would remain competitive. Sanger predicted rising earnings and steady sales volume.

Sanger received an unpleasant lesson in the workings of The Commodity Zone. One year after weaning consumers off the promotions, market share, volume, and profits had all declined. Customers had been trained to wait for a sale price. In their minds, the product was no longer worth the everyday price. Each trip down the supermarket aisle became a game of "chicken"—I'll buy when you lower your price again. Over the years, General Mills had trained its customers to watch and wait for a bargain.

I recently attempted to wrestle an Embassy Suites Hotel into The Commodity Zone. They wouldn't budge. I approached the reservations manager and said, "I'll be returning to your area next month for a 14 day visit. I can stay at the Courtyard Hotel up the road for $82 a night. Can you match that rate?"

The response was swift and sure. "I'm sorry, I won't be able to offer you that rate. Our 14 day rate is $94. May I tell you why we feel it's an excellent value?" ("I'm writing a book on this subject," I thought. "Of course you can tell me.")

She explained that they offered a full, complimentary breakfast and an evening cocktail reception. Their rooms were considerably larger than the Courtyard's, with a full-size work desk. "These are all features that I think will help you have a more productive stay."

Instead of becoming just like a Courtyard, the reservation manager painted a clear picture in my mind of what made Embassy Suites different and better than other hotels. Price is only one factor in delivering value. Many businesses now assume that their customers care only about lowest price. This assumption has led to banners declaring, "We will be not undersold," and "Low-price guarantee." Such a low-price obsession might lead eventually to another banner: "Going out of business."

Competing toe-to-toe with your lowest price competitor is lunacy. Your emphasis is diverted from quality and distinction to "How low can we go?" Delivering the lowest price requires slashing your cost and overhead. Research and development dollars are typically cut from the budget. You now produce the same product or service as everyone else. Reduced revenues make it more difficult to maintain your physical plant and to adequately reward and motivate your work force.

Competing on price usually results from an assumption—a false assumption—that price is your prospect's only concern. My United Parcel Service sales representative blindly assumed that all that mattered to me was getting it there the cheapest way. It **is** all that matters for some customers, but not for me. I'm more concerned that it gets there.

Every day, new high-volume, low-margin competitors march into town and catch the established businesses flat-footed. Most respond in knee-jerk, clone-like fashion. The popular business thinking is, "If I don't match the competitor's price, I can't compete." This book urges you *not* to match the price and, more importantly, *not* to match the product.

Your business has a choice. You can continually improve and develop your product or service in ways that help protect your price. Or you can lose your comparative and competitive edge and guarantee lowest price. It's hard to be the new, improved Boboli pizza shell while being the new, lower priced Boboli pizza shell. Customers find it hard to imagine both can occur at once.

The 7 Universal Laws of Customer Value devotes a chapter to each of the Universal Laws. It shows you how to avoid The Commodity Zone. You'll learn how to create a better product, service, and purchase experience for your customer. The Seven Universal Laws are:

1. **Defy Comparison.** Offer a product so distinct and unique that "apples to apples" comparisons no longer apply.
2. **Remove the Risk.** Can your customers say, "What do I have to lose?" Allow them to try your product before the purchase and protect their investment *after* the purchase with a money-back guarantee.
3. **Qualify Your Customers.** Price is the end-all and be-all to only *part* of the marketplace—the part you want to avoid if you'd like to be profitable.
4. **Narrow Your Offerings.** Simplify your customer's purchase decision by offering fewer options. Less is more.
5. **Tell the Truth.** Cut the hype—deliver on your promises. Your customers will become your sales force.
6. **Consistency Beats Occasional Excellence.** Be predictable, reliable, without surprise. Occasionally "wowing" them isn't as important as satisfying them every time.

7. **Keep in Touch (More than a Bill).** Stay in your customer's mind by delivering quality and value and then *reminding* your customer what you've delivered.

Any business can incorporate these timeless secrets and put them to work. Every business should revisit these seven laws regularly to ensure that they are still adding value.

Today's customers want to pay no more than is absolutely necessary. But what are they paying for? Are you delivering a better product or service than you were one year ago? Are you delivering a better product or service than your competitors? If not, you're in The Commodity Zone. You need ways to break out. Let me show you how.

Defy Comparison

Let's try an experiment. I'm going to blindfold you and take you to your local tavern. I place you on a barstool and say to the bartender, "Joe, pour this thirsty soul a Budweiser and a Miller and a Coors." You take a sip of each and then I ask you, "Tell me, which one of these tastes beechwood aged? And can you tell which glass was cold filtered? Any of the three make you feel like you're high in the Rockies?" You're stumped. They all taste the same.

Not a drinker? Instead of the bar, I'll drive you to the airport. (Let me drive—you're still blindfolded). I take you to the gate, you choose an aisle seat, I take the window. I find our seats and stow our luggage. The safety announcements begin, we start to push back from the gate, I turn to you and ask, "Which airline are we on—United, American, or Delta?" You don't have a clue. Same seats, same announcements, same miniaturized meal trays.

Can your customers tell your product blindfolded? Are you so unique and distinct that you can't be mistaken for someone else? This is the first secret of value. Create a product or service that makes price comparison impossible because your product or service defies comparison. If you

1

choose instead to provide the same product or service as everyone else, you invite your customers to stare at your price tag.

No one is granted immunity from this emerging principle of commerce. Being a household word, an established brand, means less to more people today than in any time in modern history. There was a time when a laundry detergent could proclaim, "New! More Suds!" and raise its price. Today's consumers don't fall for such foolishness. Premium prices are justified only when your product or service does a better job at meeting a customer's need or solving his or her problem.

AN APPLE BECOMES AN ORANGE

Apple's Macintosh® computer once commanded a premium price because it made computing easy. No other machine let you point a mechanical mouse to click open a file, make a drawing or delete an unwanted file by dragging it to an on-screen trashcan. Then Microsoft introduced Windows® for the competing DOS-based computer. Windows software was capable of mimicking many of the Mac's proprietary features and benefits. No longer unique, the Macintosh could no longer justify its higher prices in the marketplace. Windows had transformed Apple's winning product into an orange. Faced with declining sales, Apple chairman John Sculley ordered across-the-board price cuts on all Macs in order to compete more effectively.

Look at the software industry and you'll discover what happens when competing products act or behave alike. Customers can't tell the difference between one spreadsheet or word processing program and the next. "Feature-wise, all the different vendors are hitting 85 percent of our requirements," said corporate software buyer Steven D. Birgfield of Booz, Allen & Hamilton Inc. If all the programs can do the job, and no one vendor delivers a distinct advantage, is it any wonder the prices head for the bargain basement? Borland International's Quattro Pro®

spreadsheet program is a case study in perpetually tumbling prices. In 1990, Quattro Pro had a retail price of $495 but could be had on the streets for $99.95. By 1993, $99.95 was the *retail* price. You could buy it for $49.95. Such price cuts can build tremendous sales volume but at the cost of profits.

INNOVATION IN HIBERNATION

In many industries, new competitors have successfully grabbed the opposite end of the value stick. They create a premium product and price it accordingly. The ice cream industry is an excellent example of a business that witnessed a remarkable transformation during the 1980s. Value-priced ice cream brands in supermarket freezers tasted the same, bland and cold. Ben & Jerry's and Pillsbury's Hagen Dazs introduced ice cream so much richer and more tempting than the supermarket brands that their pint container became a popular serving for one. The super-premium ice cream category was born—higher in calories, fat, taste, and price. Supermarket brands cost about two dollars per half gallon; Ben & Jerry's typically cost two dollars a pint.

Ask today's beer drinkers, "What'll you have?," and a growing number respond with a beer that didn't exist five years ago. They call for Boston's Samuel Adams or Palo Alto's Pete's Wicked Ale or Seattle's Redhook. Microbreweries in every city have a loyal following because they're producing beers distinctive in color, body, aroma, and taste. Microbrewers have an almost counterculture appeal because they eschew traditional advertising and refuse to sell their beer in cans or use mass-brewing techniques. In an industry with overall flat sales, the microbreweries are growing at 40 percent a year.

And if you think beer drinkers have defected from well-known brands to save money, you're about to make a sobering discovery. Small breweries command a big price. My recent supermarket visit revealed that six-packs of Budweiser, Miller, and Coors were $3.99. Farther down the aisle, a six-pack of Samuel Adams and Pete's Wicked Ale had a price that many New Englanders would describe as . . . wicked high—$ 5.99.

The largest breweries have sown the seeds of the microbrewers' opportunity. Years have passed and the taste of Budweiser, Miller, and Coors hasn't changed or improved. The major breweries instead relied on humorous advertising and consumer goodwill to fuel growth. Sales trends indicate it hasn't been enough.

It's in the industries where innovation is in hibernation that opportunities abound. When you produce something unique, useful, and bound to delight, you're on your way to higher profits.

DEFYING COMPARISON IN THE AIR

The best known of the airlines spawned from the deregulation of the 1980s is Texas-based Southwest. Its no-frills, low-fare service has been widely imitated by the larger carriers, including United and Continental. But commercial aviation has its own lesser-known version of a microbrewer—Midwest Express Airlines. When you step on board one of their planes, you happily discover that Midwest Express soars through the blindfold test. As soon as you're seated, you notice that there's actually some space between your arms and the armrests. Your sense of touch appreciates the leatherbound seat.

Upon take-off, your nose gets a surprise—the sweet aroma of chocolate chip cookies. Once your blindfold is removed, you can enjoy the newspaper you were offered at the check-in gate. When Midwest Express Airlines promises "the best care in the air," they ascend beyond the customer's Commodity Zone.

The airline has its roots in private aviation. Prior to 1984, it served as a charter service for Kimberly-Clark Corporation's mobile executives. Having its own fleet of planes allowed Kimberly-Clark to shuttle its managers from plant to plant with greater comfort and efficiency.

The managers loved the small touches, the larger seats, and the good food so difficult to find on commercial flights.

Midwest Express chairman Timothy E. Hoeksema explains the reason for an in-house airline: "Many Kimberly-Clark people were experiencing difficulty with air travel at the time. Service was lousy, schedules were skimpy. It was easy to figure out that if we were unhappy, lots of other people were too." Hoeksema continues, "When you have an industry with dissatisfied customers, you have a business opportunity."

From day one, Midwest Express Airlines dared to be different. While other airlines were cramming more seats into each aircraft, Midwest Express was removing seats so that no passenger was ever stuck in the middle.

In an era when most airlines consider a bag of peanuts a full course meal, Midwest Express continues to serve food better than Mama used to make. Meals include a grilled chicken cold plate or filet mignon. This airline spends more than $10 per passenger on food. What about the competition? In the first quarter of 1994, American Airlines spent $6.20 per passenger, down from a 1991 figure of $6.74; United, $4.86; US Air, $2.64; and Southwest—13 cents. No wonder disembarking passengers greet their families, "I missed you. When can we eat?"

Recognition is finally coming Midwest's way. *Consumer Reports Travel Letter* has identified Midwest Express as the best airline in the country in four consecutive rating periods. *Conde Nast Traveler* provided similar recognition in its three most recent surveys.

What about price? Are Midwest Express fares in the stratosphere? Midwest offers competitive fares but avoids leading the pack into profit-draining fare wars. When it enters a new market, it does so carefully, avoiding routes already occupied by bargain basement carriers. Pricing, research, and yield management groups work closely together to balance competitive pricing with healthy revenues. While major carriers fly in and out of the red, Midwest has been consistently profitable since 1987.

Meanwhile, other airlines continue to imitate each other's moves: less food, "lite" fares, wage concessions, cramped seating, and a partly cloudy profit forecast. Veteran air travelers fear that eventually, the question asked at the ticket counter will not be "Window or aisle?" but, "Would you like to sit or stand?"

MAKING IT BETTER

Every day, companies choose either to compete on price or to create a product of the highest quality. Any product or service can be improved and made more valuable. W. L. Gore & Associates, Inc., best known for its Gore-Tex® fabric, produces a dental floss that moves smoothly between teeth and gums, without that annoying shredding present in most nylon-based flosses.

In 1990, Gore approached the two largest floss sellers, Johnson & Johnson and Colgate-Palmolive, hoping to gain distribution for its innovative product. Neither expressed interest. Gore went it alone. Today, Glide Mint® generates more retail dollars than any floss product sold in the United States. Glide® unflavored is fourth on the list out of 176 floss products available. Once again, some customers are willing to pay more for something better. My local drugstore sells 55 yards of Glide for $3.67. Fifty yards of Johnson & Johnson's nylon floss cost $1.49.

Down the street, the local tire dealer is defying comparison. Goodyear Tire & Rubber decided that tires need not be commodities and developed the Aquatred®, a premium priced road-hugger which more effectively reduces hydroplaning than its lower priced counterparts. The average Aquatred retails for over $90, 10 percent more than Goodyear's previous top-of-the-line mass market tire.

Service businesses make a similar choice. Professional speaker Joel Weldon's business philosophy is, "Find out what everyone else is doing and then don't do it." If you want a canned talk on management, sales, customer service, or increased personal effectiveness, Joel's *not* your man. He's found his clients are *not* interested in him giving a "canned" talk, or the same presentation as he did to his last audience. They want a totally customized and focused message.

Joel adds value by being better prepared for your group than anyone you've ever heard. He spends an average of 50 hours of preparation time for every 4 hour seminar. His new clients are surprised at the number of background questions he asks about their organization. He reads everything he can get his hands on, learning industry lingo, history and trends. As a result, Weldon is one of the highest paid non-celebrity speakers in the United States.

TAKING THE HIGH ROAD

Television talk show host Oprah Winfrey is one of the world's best-known celebrities and is currently America's highest-paid entertainer. In 1986, the *Oprah Winfrey Show* gained national syndication and it didn't take long for Oprah's ratings to rise above the competition. Her down-to-earth manner and compelling interviewing style attracted legions of loyal fans. Rival talk-show host Maury Povich describes the talk-show landscape prior to *The Oprah Winfrey Show:* "Nobody was talking about their own problems like Oprah . . . Oprah opened up a lot of new windows for viewers because they could empathize with her."

She also did the little things that defied comparison. If an author was appearing on the show, she actually knew the book. The whole book. After every show taping, she spent about 45 minutes saying goodbye to the more than 250 people who came to watch the show. It's not in the job description, but it does create audience loyalty and a lasting memory.

Along came the Oprah impersonators, each one gunning for her huge daytime audience. Each new talk-show host chose a Winfrey-like format, with a vocal studio audience, live call-ins, and free flowing discussion. But this new generation of on-air discussions would never be mistaken for parliamentary debate. *Robert's Rules of Order* were out of order. Angry, victimized guests vented their wrath on the stranger or relative just one chair away. The new talk show hosts egged their guests on to the psychological breaking point.

These new shows and topics were popular, particularly with young viewers. Oprah was not above the fray. She took her turn refereeing the verbal mudslinging from guests. The pressure was on because her daytime ratings domination was at risk. By mid-1994, all the shows, including Oprah's, were behaving alike. Oprah no longer defied comparison.

The summer of 1994 was Oprah's time for soul-searching. After reading an article by sociologist Vicki Abt which lambasted all talk shows, including hers, as "voyeuristic titillation," Abt was invited on the show as a guest. Shortly thereafter, Oprah changed course. She began a conscious effort to improve the quality of the information presented on her show. Said Winfrey, "I cannot listen to people blaming their mothers for another year. I have to move on."

She did. Channel surfing on a typical weekday reveals a marked difference in tone and content between *The Oprah Winfrey Show* and the rest of the pack. While other talk-show hosts continue to behave like referees for the World Wrestling Federation, Oprah's setting herself apart by taking the high road. The jury's still out on the ratings impact of this strategy, but John Garwood of Oprah affiliate WPLG in Miami commends the move: "Oprah is a great creative force in talk shows, and she may be doing exactly the right thing to differentiate herself in the future."

SAME BIC®—DIFFERENT BLADE

While watching television the other day, a brief advertisement proclaimed, "Bic pens—still 19 cents." "Still 19 cents? How can that be?," I wondered. "They were 19 cents when I was in grade school!"

Then I thought, "Is this something Bic should be proud of? Couldn't the pen have been improved and commanded a higher price during those 30 years? Is the customer best served by a product stuck in a time warp?"

The Gillette Company offers an interesting contrast. Their bestselling razor blade of 30 years ago has been replaced and upgraded four times. In 1971, Gillette introduced the Trac II®, with two blades positioned in a single cartridge. 1977 marked the arrival of Atra®, also with twin blades, but in a new, pivoting head.

In 1990, Atra was upstaged by one of the most successful product launches in history, the Sensor® shaving system. Since Sensor's introduction, Gillette's total razor and blade sales have increased an impressive 54 percent in the United States and 71 percent worldwide. But the world's largest blade company didn't rest there. In 1993–94, SensorExcel® appeared, with a design similar to the original Sensor, but adding five microfins below the twin blades, which stretch the beard before it meets its doom.

Each generation of blade, or "shaving systems" as Gillette calls them, is more effective and more profitable than its predecessor. Sensor Excel cartridges are approximately 15 percent more expensive than the Sensor blades. Sensor cartridges are priced approximately 15 percent higher than the Atra, and so forth. "The best measure of a company is not what it's accomplished, but how well it's improved the prospects for the future," says Alfred Zeinen, chairman and chief executive of The Gillette Company.

Are you more like Bic or Gillette? Are you maintaining your product or service like Bic, keeping it in a perpetual holding pattern? Or like Gillette, have you chosen to acclimate your customers to higher prices by creating a more valuable product or service? The dangers in being a Bic are:

- There's always some competitor lurking in the shadows ready to offer an 18-cent pen.
- Volume drives your profits. You must sell oceanliners full of your product to prevent your business from becoming the Titanic.

- A competitor builds a better mousetrap than you and captures a big chunk of your customer base. You can't compete because your tiny profits leave no room for research and development.

The benefits of emulating Gillette are:

- Customers enjoy an ever-improving product. Their problem is solved, time is saved, or experience made more pleasurable.
- Profit margins are easier to maintain because you avoid price wars. When nothing compares to what you sell, it's easier to sell it at a higher price.

Most razor blade makers, brewers, automobile tire manufacturers, professional speakers, commercial airlines, and talk-show hosts produce their industry's equivalent of a 19-cent pen and then wonder why customers refuse to pay more than 19 cents. It's because marketing smoke and mirrors no longer works. Without a distinctively better product, the customer holds out for a sale.

HOW ABOUT YOUR LINE?

Say we place your product or service in a police line-up with four of your competitors. Your prospect looks through the glass and the detective says, "OK, which one will it be?" Do you stand out as the clear choice? Or do you look like one of five quintuplets? The first secret to avoiding price wars is to avoid being mistaken for your competition. Price is only one variable in the equation of value; the better your product or service, the more you diminish its importance in the equation.

Here are some questions and an exercise that will help you begin to defy comparison:

1. A prospect calls you on the telephone. Describe your product or service to the prospect in less than 30 seconds. Write your description below.

_____

_____

_____

_____

_____

_____

_____

_____

_____

2. List three ways that your product or service defies comparison; i.e., is different and better than your competition.

_____

_____

_____

_____

_____

_____

3. Your prospect says, "I can buy it cheaper from someone else. Why I should I pay more for what you're selling?" How would you respond?

_____

_____

_____

_____

_____

_____

_____

4. What recent improvements have you made to your
product or service (within the past 12 months)?

_____

_____

_____

_____

_____

_____

_____

_____

5. Do you know these improvements please your
customers? How do you know (focus groups,
surveys, phone conversations)?

_____

_____

_____

_____

_____

_____

_____

_____

6. What changes or improvements have your competitors made in the past 12 months?

_____

_____

_____

_____

_____

_____

7. Name three ways you plan to defy comparison (improve your product or service) over the next 12 months.

_____

_____

_____

_____

_____

_____

8. How will you communicate these improvements to your prospects and customers?

_____

_____

_____

_____

_____

_____

Remove the Risk

Looking through the Sunday newspaper, I saw an advertisement for an Oreck vacuum cleaner. "Call us for a free brochure describing our eight-pound wonder." I called. The Oreck representative pleasantly tried to talk me out of the brochure and into a free 15-day, in-home trial. It was clear that she was on a mission to get that eight-pound sensation into my hands.

She wasn't trying to sell it. She wanted me to *try* it. There's a world of difference. Colorful brochures and spectacular specifications don't sell your product. Your product should sell itself. Allowing prospects to be users is a sure-fire way to add value.

Take this book, for example. If you're in a bookstore right now and haven't yet made a purchase decision, take your time. Look through all seven chapters and begin to read at random. If the words don't hold your interest, if the ideas aren't valuable, don't buy this book.

Strange advice? Not when you have something worthwhile to sell. When you're confident that your product has merit, you know that a free trial will create the sale rather than kill it. That's why Oreck wants me to try the vacuum cleaner. They know that once I do, I won't want to ship it back.

Free trials are an important weapon in a commodity-laden marketplace. It's the best way to prove that your product is better and different than the rest. In describing a recent breakfast cereal sampling promotion, General Mills spokeswoman Katherine Newton said, "Sampling is a key to our business, [and part of] . . . a major effort to lure new cereal lovers. . ."

Rick Vancisin, of Gorton's of Gloucester, points out, "The biggest hurdle with anything new is getting customers to take the chance. Sampling can help you overcome that hurdle." But, Vancisin advises, "Sampling is expensive. It works only if you have a really good and unique product."

Free sampling saved one product from an early demise. Debbi Fields opened her first Mrs. Fields® Cookies stand in Palo Alto, California in 1977. She had a great recipe, high hopes, and no customers. She decided to stop selling the cookies and instead concentrate on giving the product away. Mrs. Fields cut up some of those tasty, tempting creations, placed them on a serving tray, and invited her prospects to dig in. The results were immediate and legendary. Mrs. Fields grew from that one small stand to hundreds of locations throughout the United States and Great Britain.

Without a demonstration or a no-risk chance to try, new products aren't even noticed. Every day, in stores across the country, sales are lost because demonstrations don't occur. Computer departments in superstores are a notorious example. Walk down the aisle and take a look at the monitors. The screens are either blank or beckon, "Please enter password." How can you enter a password you don't know? Without a demonstration, the price tag seems too steep, the risk too high. No sale.

Suppose you owned the computer store. You could load the most commonly used software into your powerful, state-of-the-art machines. You and your staff could invite customers to get behind the keyboard and test drive applications they use every day on their own, slower machines. Won't you make more sales?

Other opportunities are missed all the time. Tourists frequently stop in front of unfamiliar restaurants and look at the menu posted on the wall. Most passersby read it but keep walking. What if someone from the restaurant came outside and gave those tourists a taste of what's inside? If the food is outstanding, hungry visitors follow their taste buds to a table or a booth.

Plenty of today's smart marketers are removing the risk. Ralph Lauren wants you to try his Polo Sport Face Fitness Moisturizer® for two weeks for free, without obligation. He's confident you'll be "hooked" and come back for more. L. L. Bean will help you hook a fish. But before you buy that fly rod, you're welcome to try it. There's a small drainage pond directly behind the store ideal for a quick trial "cast."

L. L. Bean recognizes this developing trend in product sampling and intends to bring the great outdoors inside its retail store. Plans are in the works for a major expansion, including a rain room to test waterproof gear, a small demonstration rink for rollerbladers, and an indoor trout pond for avid fishermen.

SELLING AT RETAIL—WORTH THE PRICE

Risk removal adds value that can help you justify a full retail price. You might offer the same product as your competition, but decide that you're the only one willing to provide a no obligation trial. Learningsmith, a New England-based retailer of educational products, sells almost all its merchandise at suggested retail price, a practice rarely seen in today's how-low-can-you-go marketplace. "We sell at full retail because we work hard to earn it. We bring more value to the transaction," explains Leticia Fleischer, Learningsmith's director of marketing and visual presentation. "If you make it easy to see, ask, and try, you make it easy to buy."

Two years ago, Learningsmith proved its point. My son, Kevin, needed some remedial work in mathematics. He and I made a field trip to our local shopping mall in search of Math Blaster, a popular software program. My goal was to buy Math Blaster at the lowest possible price. Our first stop was to New England discounter Lechmere. The price? $44.95. It seemed too high. The next stop was Learningsmith. Their price was $49.95. "They've got to be kidding!" I thought. Before I could move on, a Learningsmith sales representative approached Kevin and said, "We have another program called Math Ace. Do you want to try it?"

Kevin sat down at one of the store's computers and started putting the program through its paces. Within two minutes, he turned to me and said, "This is great, Dad!"

Sold. I never asked about the price. The store had proven that my son would use the program. At Lechmere, software programs are sold based on what's written on the box. Learningsmith had discovered a way to take the program out of the box and put it into my son's hands.

Learningsmith's store offerings are arranged in clusters, by product type. Educational videos play in one corner of the store; astronomy, geography, board games, and computer software each have their own areas. Instead of the products being stacked on the shelves, many, like Math Ace, are "out of the box," so that young and curious minds can discover the enjoyment and wonder of the products. This hands-on experience increases the chances they'll head for the cash register before they head for the exit.

Marshall Smith, founder of Learningsmith, learned the value of the free trial at his earlier retail start-up, Paperback Booksmith. A bookstore's vitality depends on consumers' ability to browse through the shelves and "test drive" as many books as they'd like. Smith points out, "Some people walk into a bookstore knowing exactly what they want. However, we noticed that a large portion of our customers showed up just to browse and walked out with some books under their arm. I knew this concept could be applied in a new arena." The adaptation is in evidence every day in any of Learningsmith's 31 stores.

Jim Hackett, vice-president of Market Source, echoes Smith's comments. He points out that 70 percent of shoppers head to the mall without a specific destination or purchase in mind. What happens *inside* the store often drives the purchase decision.

BRINGING NATURE TO LIFE

Point-of-purchase displays can also create a sampling of the product. Northword Press of Minocqua, Wisconsin, was once a modest business selling nature calendars and books. In 1990, it acquired the rights to sell Nature Music Audios from Canada. The performers on these cassettes and CDs presented a unique marketing problem. As Northword's Jim Olsen says, "We couldn't send the loons and the wolves out on tour."

Olsen noticed that the stores having the most success selling the tapes were the ones playing them in the store. He thought sales could be increased if Northword could devise a way to make a demonstration easy.

He sought help from CD equipment manufacturers but they showed little interest. After much trial-and-error, he and a colleague developed a display unit that consisted of a logic chip, a circuit board, two speakers, a CD player and a master CD which contained sixty-second samples of each available cassette/CD title. The customer approached the display, touched a panel displaying the cover art of a desired title, and within seconds heard a one-minute sample in full digital sound.

Olsen says the displays sent sales soaring. In five years, annual company sales have grown from $3.5 million to $40 million. Four thousand of these displays are currently in the field.

WHY REMOVE THE RISK?

There are several trends driving customers' risk aversion:

- Incomes aren't rising as fast as the prices of some goods. For example, in inflation-adjusted dollars, the cost of today's automobile takes a bigger chunk of the customer's paycheck than at any time in modern history. Buying a lemon becomes an even costlier mistake, making customers more careful than ever.

- Consumers are buying for keeps. As purchasers mature, they recognize that high-quality goods are a better value. A cheap price is only cheap until the product breaks down.

Since you're facing a more cautious consumer, you can use a two-pronged strategy to remove the risk:

1. Offer a free trial or demonstration *before* the purchase decision.

2. Give the customer his/her money back *after* the purchase if not totally satisfied.

The more unusual a money-back guarantee is in your industry, the more effective your offer will be. You'll grab your customer's attention and improve your ability to compete. Money-back guarantees have recently been introduced into a wide variety of industries: motion pictures, hospitality, professional speaking, publishing, and even the college classroom. Consider these examples:

Twentieth Century Fox was the first major film studio to back up its product with a guarantee. It removed the risk by making a moviegoing offer hard to refuse. On November 25, 1994, the following advertisement ran in major newspapers nationwide:

> Twentieth Century Fox
> is proud to invite you
> to experience the extraordinary
> motion picture
> "Miracle on 34th Street."
> Audiences have seen it
> and loved it, and we
> guarantee you will too.

> So, from now until Sunday,
> we invite you to go see this movie,
> and if you do not agree,
> just mail in your ticket stub
> and we will refund your price of admission.

What if we create an even bolder offer? Imagine you owned a movie theater and offered a money-back guarantee. What if customers could return to the ticket window at any time during the movie and ask for their money back? Would you be adding value? Would you have a competitive advantage? Would you show better movies? And would your customers be more satisfied?

Perhaps you think I've lost my marbles and that your movie theater would lose its shirt. Maybe not. When you imagine yourself in a money-back world, you probably dwell on expected losses. But if you offer a high-quality product, you'll generate far more additional business than what you'll pay out in losses—especially if none of your competitors dares make such an offer.

Twentieth Century Fox held its money-back results close to its vest. By contrast, Promus Co. proudly announced its winning hand—a $10 million hand. The Memphis-based hotel and gaming operator wanted to lure more customers to its Hampton Inns hotels. Promus began offering full refunds to any customers who were dissatisfied with their stays. In 1993, only one tenth of one percent of guests asked for a refund. The chain paid out $1.1 million in refunds, but Promus officials estimate the program brought in an additional $11 million in revenue that same year.

Promus chief executive Michael Rose contends the guarantee is a more profitable strategy than attracting customers through discounted room rates. "I think discounting is a very long-term defeatist strategy and it's not cyclical. You've told your customers that your products are not worth as much as they're paying."

Likewise, professional speaker Joel Weldon guarantees the satisfaction of every one of his presentations. He typically speaks to a large corporate audience. Every person who attends Joel's talk completes an evaluation form, ranking the presentation on a 1 to 10 scale, 1 being awful and 10 terrific. Joel's not paid for any evaluation that comes back with a ranking lower than a 7. For example, if 100 people attend his presentation and two attendees rank it lower than a 7, the client pays only 98 percent of the agreed-upon fee.

Joel says, "Imagine yourself offering a similar guarantee. Think how much harder you'd work at being good." Joel's not giving back much money. He estimates that in the past 22 years, only four-tenths of one per cent of his total revenues were refunded under the guarantee. What he *is* doing is setting himself apart from other speakers by removing the risk to the meeting planner or corporation that hires him.

USC business professor Richard Chase is another trailblazer. In his marketing course, he has always advocated a money-back guarantee. In 1991, he started offering one. Any student dissatisfied with the quality of his teaching could ask for a refund, $250 in tuition and $100 towards books. Standing to lose more than $20,000 if all his students took refunds, Chase said, "I have to do a gut check and say, 'Can I do what I promised?' . . . It forces me to really get my act together." Two-thirds of the way through the semester, students said Chase was delivering the goods. "He's dynamic. He uses a lot of different media. He expresses himself well," said graduate student Heidi Fillo. "I haven't heard of anybody say they are [thinking of asking for a refund]."

Chase's offer also improved his business. The same course offered before the guarantee attracted 25 students. Post-guarantee, 65 students enrolled.

Author Sharyn Wolf thought a guarantee might be just what she needed to get her book noticed. Anyone who bought *Guerrilla Dating Tactics* was guaranteed they would learn skills that would get them a date. If after a year the social calendar was still empty, his or her money would be refunded.

MAKING IT EASY

The trade journal, *Profit-building Strategies,* argues that once interested buyers see a long list of exceptions or limitations to the guarantee, they're likely to turn to a competing product with more realistic promises. "It's often better for a company to offer a good-faith guarantee instead of a time-limited, money-back guarantee that is accompanied by a litany of exceptions and limitations."

A well-designed guarantee will create future goodwill and repeat business. Clumsy rules and regulations can drive customers away for good.

Service guarantees deliver the most value when they are:

- ✔ *Unconditional.* Do not split hairs or pro-rate your refund. If the product fails to meet expectations, bite the bullet and offer the *full* money back.
- ✔ *Easy to understand.* Hampton Inns' guarantee was direct and plain. If you're dissatisfied for any reason, your money is refunded.
- ✔ *Easy to invoke.* Your customer shouldn't be required to fill out 23 forms in triplicate and endure a cross-examination from your company's legal counsel.
- ✔ *Easy to collect.* Money should be returned on-the-spot if that's the customer's wish.

PRODUCT GUARANTEES

You might be convinced that service guarantees help make more sales and instill consumer confidence. Shouldn't products (durables) also carry their own money-back guarantee? Won't product guarantees make these products stand alone in the marketplace and help fuel more sales? Volkswagen USA discovered that product guarantees don't always create the desired results.

In 1991, Volkswagen offered buyers of their Passat sedan a 30-day or 3,000-mile guarantee. The guarantee boosted recognition of the car, but, according to a VW spokeswoman, did little to increase sales. Most buyers who kept the cars would have bought them anyway. VW also had to contend with those cars returned under the guarantee. They were no longer new and, like almost all other automobiles, depreciated rapidly. Volkswagen USA suspended the program after three months.

American automaker Saturn is having a better experience. It continues to offer a one-month, 1,500-mile money-back guarantee. "We've offered it since day one, feeling that it was an important marketing tool for an upstart automobile with no track record," says Saturn spokesman Greg Martin. "We continue to offer the guarantee but find it's rarely invoked." No one at Saturn claimed that the money-back guarantee was creating additional sales. It's simply another facet of a customer-friendly sales approach.

Covering the Back End

Before instituting a product guarantee, decide what you're going to do with any returned merchandise. IBM offers a 30-day, money-back guarantee on its computers sold directly to consumers. Computers returned under the guarantee are placed in an IBM factory outlet store in North Carolina.

If you sell items priced more modestly than computers or cars, you're a better candidate for a product guarantee. Lower ticket items are far easier to restock, reshelve, and re-sell at full retail price. For example, both L. L. Bean and Lands' End will replace or refund the purchase price of any article which fails to meet a customer's expectations. This process benefits the stores in several ways:

- Returned goods help alert these companies to manufacturing defects that might otherwise go undetected.
- The customer goodwill and increased sales engendered by this guarantee more than make up for unscrupulous customers who might use the store's promise to "rent" rather than "buy" needed items.
- The guarantee is a core value in both establishments, instilling pride and a sense of purpose in the workforce. Both companies prominently display the guarantee: in every Lands' End catalog and on the large sign inside the L. L. Bean store in Freeport, Maine.

Low-Price Guarantee?

The best guarantees reinforce the value you provide, not the price your customer pays. Notice that Hampton Inns, Joel Weldon, Professor Chase, Sharyn Wolf, and Saturn are offering *results,* not the lowest price. Guaranteeing the lowest price directs the purchaser to the wrong side of the value equation.

Advertising giant J. Walter Thompson used a low-price guarantee as a clever way to generate new business. The company sent letters to clients of other advertising agencies and media buying services offering to beat their current agency's spot-television costs by 15 percent or they would service the account for free for six months. The guarantee is constructed solely around cost (we can do it cheaper) rather than quality (we can do it better). This proposal had limited success in producing new business.

Are you facing fierce competition? Resist the temptation to focus on guaranteed lowest price. It's a trap. When you promote yourself as the low-price leader, you're in the consumer education business, teaching your prospects the wrong lesson. Instead, guarantee complete satisfaction with the purchase or their money back.

If you have a great product but not-so-great sales, a free trial may be just what you need. Today's consumer is unwilling to gamble on an unknown product or service. Think of ways that you can help your prospects try before they buy.

Here's an example. United Gilsonite Laboratories (UGL) wants customers to take its Drylok® waterproofing paint home and apply it to their basement walls. To prove the product's effectiveness, UGL displays a single cinder block near the checkout line in hundreds of hardware stores. One half of the block is painted with Drylok, the other side is left untreated. A pump continuously circulates water through the block, soaking the untreated side but creating no dampening effect on the Drylok side. Customers can touch the results and buy with greater confidence. Some questions for your consideration follow.

> If you have a great product but not-so-great sales, a free trial may be just what you need. Today's consumer is unwilling to gamble on an unknown product or service. Think of ways that you can help your prospects try before they buy.

1. What product or service do you offer that's like Drylok, i.e., it works, but your customers don't know it?

_____

_____

_____

_____

_____

2. How can you demonstrate this product or service to a wary buyer?

_____

_____

_____

_____

_____

3. For what *length of time* will you allow your prospect to try out your product or service?

_____

_____

4. Will you offer a money-back guarantee?

_____

5. Will you *advertise* your money-back guarantee? If so, how?

_____

_____

_____

_____

_____

6. Will you offer a *lifetime* guarantee?

_____

_____

7. What will you do with returned merchandise?

_____

_____

_____

_____

_____

_____

8. If your customers are not completely satisfied, can they choose between getting their money back or receiving a replacement product?

_____

_____

_____

_____

_____

9. I'll incorporate these changes by _____ .

THIRD

Qualify Your Customers

"There's nothing like the first after-breakfast cigar, if it's a good one and this new lot have the right mellow flavor. They're a great bargain, too. I got them dead cheap."

James Tyrone, in Eugene O'Neil's Long Day's Journey Into Night

James Tyrone knows a good cigar, but more importantly, he can always smell a bargain. Every decision has a price; he insists that it be a low one. His summer home is a bit run down, but it was a good deal. He provides domestic care for his sickly wife, Mary, but because he's unwilling to pay the going wage, the help isn't particularly helpful. When Mary was pregnant with their youngest son, Edmund, he sent for the "hotel doctor," who charged him one dollar, not one of those, "five-dollars-to-look-at-your-tongue-fellows." In the final act, when Edmund enters the living room, his father chastises him for leaving the hallway light on: "There's no reason to have the house ablaze with electricity at this time of night, burning up money."

Some of today's consumers are just like James Tyrone. Words like "Sale of the Century," "Drastic Reductions," and "Everything Must Go" are music to their ears. Try speaking to them about your product being of higher quality, or being more durable, or delivering better results, and they'll interrupt you—"How much?"

Estimates vary on the percentage of customers who fit the Tyrone mold. Author Tom Winninger cites a 27 percent figure. Research from the Yankee Group (Boston, MA) reveals that 16 percent of all American households recently switched long-distance carriers, apparently in search of the lowest price. Whatever the percentage, these customers are myopic. They understand today's lowest price but fail to grasp the longer term concept of *lowest cost*.

TOTAL COST—CUSTOMERS WITH A FUTURE

Johnson & Dix supplies heating oil to thousands of homes in New Hampshire and Vermont. When prospects call and ask, "What's your price today?," they're quoted a competitive price, but it's probably not the lowest price in town. Every New England community has that one-person discount oil business whose only overhead is the delivery truck parked in the front yard.

Johnson & Dix doesn't attract the price shopper. Their loyal customers understand the concept of total cost. They recognize the long-term price of neglecting their furnace and are willing to invest in an annual cleaning. Paying a few additional pennies a gallon assures that, if and when their furnace breaks down, a Johnson & Dix technician will arrive with the parts and the knowledge to fix the problem. A total cost-oriented customer will pay for reliability and experience before the reliability and experience are needed; the price customer thinks only of today.

Action Automation & Controls sells machine parts for manufacturing equipment on a production line. They are *not* the cheapest source of goods, but have convinced their customers that price and cost are not the same. A cheap part that's "on its way" is very expensive. Action minimizes its customers' downtime by maintaining an inventory of the most commonly needed parts and getting them to customers faster than their discount competitors. Most parts suppliers wait for the UPS truck to deliver their incoming inventory. Not Action. Action's president, Bob Pompei, made arrangements so that one of his employees can pick up their packages at the UPS terminal, allowing them to turn around more orders on a same-day basis.

There are plenty of assembly lines that will never be equipped with Action's parts because the purchasing agent thinks only of today's price, not the downstream value of speed and reliability.

THE FIELD TRIP

When I was in the fifth grade, our class took the bus into downtown Scranton, Pennsylvania, and visited Barton's Furniture. The store owner greeted us and then told us what our parents should look for in a well-constructed piece of furniture. He tipped a couch on its side and showed us how a solid frame is built. He then removed the cushions and showed us the design of a high-quality seating section. This was furniture designed for a lifetime. The other kids seemed uninterested, but I was fascinated by his enthusiasm for what he sold.

His presentation would probably hold little interest to many of today's furniture buyers. A long-term product and relationship would be incomprehensible to them. They wait until no relationship is possible—for the going-out-of-business sale.

Customer service gurus continually remind us, "The customer is always right." Don't believe it. Some customers are *not* right for you. You cannot add value for a customer whose sole purpose is to get you to subtract from your price. Some customers:

- Define value based solely on your product's price.
- Continually dash from supplier to supplier looking for the best possible deal.
- Don't pay their bills.

In *Price Wars,* Tom Winninger offers an example of a purchase decision that, according to his own estimate, over a quarter of the market doesn't understand:

A paint company sells a premium product with tremendous "hideability," "scrub-ability," and "coverability." The paint sells for $15 a gallon. Competing paints sell for $12 a gallon, but the more expensive paint is guaranteed to stay on the house for twice as long. *The customer you want* reasons, "If I buy $300 worth of paint (25 gallons) and the paint is guaranteed to stay on my house for just 5 years, why not spend $75 more and get a paint that's guaranteed to stay on my house for 10 years?"

Spend $75 more? This is heresy to the price shopper. Why would anyone spend more on paint? The total cost customer gets it. The price shopper never will. Over a span of 10 years, the price shopper shells out $600 for the cheaper paint *plus* has to paint his house twice rather than once. The total cost shopper pays $375 dollars once. He paints his house once. He pays more up front, but saves time and money downstream.

Successful businesses are built on the foundation of solid, longlasting customer relationships. Like a carefree young bachelor, some customers aren't interested in a relationship. Why shouldn't you feel the same? There are at least four reasons:

1. Because loyal customers are more profitable. The longer they stay, the more you make. In the *Harvard Business Review,* Frederick F. Reichheld and W. Earl Sasser, Jr., surveyed four disparate industries and discovered that customer longevity was the key to higher profitably. For example, the average credit card company spends $51 to recruit a newcomer and set up an account. It's not until year five that the company makes a commensurate annual profit from the account. In every subsequent year, the profit grows.

For one auto service company surveyed, the expected profit from a fourth-year customer is more than triple the profit that same customer generated in the first year. Profits flow from confidence. As a customer develops a relationship with a business, he or she tends to use its services more frequently. The fixed cost of setting up an account is a one-time charge incurred only in that first year.

2. Because loyal customers become your secret salesforce. No one sells your product or service as effectively as your satisfied customers. Their credibility with friends, neighbors, or business colleagues is unquestioned. They send qualified prospects your way, negating the need for mass advertising and marketing.

3. Because loyal customers are an invaluable source of information. Most are happy to tell you how you can continue to please them. They can help you design future products and services. Columnist Michael Schrage points out, "Companies must learn that their best customers aren't just the ones that generate the most profit, but also the ones that inspire the best ideas and innovations."

4. Because loyal customers aren't as price sensitive as the "James Tyrones." According to Reichheld and Sasser, Jr.'s research, "Many people will pay more to stay in a hotel they know or go to a doctor they trust than to take a chance on a less expensive competitor." Our own clients' experience, including Johnson & Dix and Action Automation, supports their point.

Still need proof? Use your own experience as a guide. Unless you live in a cave and are without a telephone, you've received dozens of calls from long-distance carriers promising you the moon. You probably sent them away with no sale. Most customers need more than a lower price to motivate a change in suppliers. If prices are comparable, they wait until their present supplier stumbles before considering a switch. Most customers stick with what works.

Not so for the "spinners." These are the subscribers without loyalty. Like Ruth Holder. She was using AT&T for her long-distance calls. Then MCI called offering frequent flier miles. She switched. But then AT&T called and mailed her a $75 check to win back her business. It worked. Until

MCI called. MCI offered her 50 percent off her calls for the next six months. She accepted. Are you still with me? The story's not over.

Holder says, "I recently got a call from AT&T offering to pay me $75 plus give me 50 percent off my bill for the next six months. I haven't (switched) yet. But I'm thinking about it."

Holder is one of the 16 million households that changed long-distance carriers at least once between mid-1993 and mid-1994. Yankee Group's figures for the most recent 12 months indicate this group grew to 19 million. The questions arise: Will long distance carriers attempt to retain *every* subscriber's business? Isn't there a better way to inspire loyalty? Jay Mixter of Customer Development Corporation warns, "As a general rule, the more people were incentivized to buy, the less loyal they're going to be and the more you're going to have to spend to keep them as a customer."

LOSING CUSTOMERS ON PURPOSE

Frederick Reichheld and W. Earl Sasser, Jr., argue that your goal should be zero customer defections. They claim it's the key to higher profits. Columnist Michael Schrage urges you to fire your customers; not all of them, just the 10 to 15 percent who don't make you money or lack useful information or innovative ideas.

Go with Schrage. Unless you do a superb job qualifying your customers up front, you should *want* some of your current customers to defect. We see our clients spending inordinate amounts of time attempting to mollify a small percentage of their customers. These are the customers always looking for that profit-killing discount, or the people who are verbally berating our client's customer service staff. Where is it written that you have to do business with nasty people?

Many of our clients are perpetually dunning the same customers. Yet once their account is paid, they go right back to doing business with them. Delinquent accounts are a financial drain on any business, especially the cash-starved entrepreneur. Too many businesses strive for zero defections when, as Michael Schrage argues, they'd be better off if some of their customers *did* defect.

Even the long-distance carriers are learning that not all defections are bad news. "Marketing science has come of age. It's thrown a monkey wrench into some long-held beliefs, like that every customer is worth fighting for," says John Skalko of AT&T's Consumer Communication Service unit. "We no longer match every competitive offer dangled in front of every one of our customers. Our research indicates that if a customer has switched carriers several times in the past year and has low monthly call volume, it's not profitable to match a competitor's offer."

AT&T, MCI, and Sprint are still paying the price for their earlier unfocused efforts to steal each other's customers. Learn from their experience. When low price is your calling card, you attract truckloads of customers ready to bolt the first time a competitor waves another dollar bill in their direction.

A Better Courtship, a Longer Marriage

Focus on the quality of the customers you attract. They should be as interested in a relationship as you. Only after you improve the quality of your customers should you strive for zero defections. The best way to improve the quality of your customer base is to qualify your prospects *before* they become customers.

Let's splash a cold bucket of reality on this discussion. If you're starting a new business, and are starved for cash, your top priority is to find customers—*any* customers. Don't risk your fledgling enterprise on the notion that only the highest quality customers are worth the effort. Start qualifying customers once you're experiencing consistent growth. As one of my most successful clients told me, "We find ourselves focusing more and more time qualifying our prospects. But when I first started out, we'd do business with anyone who breathed."

HOW TO QUALIFY: ASK GOOD QUESTIONS

If you want to learn how to qualify a customer, consider a visit to your local Saturn dealer. Play the role of the car shopper and watch what happens. The Neanderthal approach to car buying is: kick the tires, take the test drive, make the offer. Not so fast. Before you get near the tires or behind the wheel, Saturn's sales consultant will interview you and explain what the car can and cannot do. Have a husband and two young kids? Sounds like a good match-up. Need a vehicle to transport the offensive line of your college football team? You're in the wrong place.

Good questions help you and the sales consultant decide if a relationship is possible; not a sale, a relationship. A skilled Saturn consultant wants to learn as much about you as you want to learn about Saturn. You'll be told that the Saturn dealer is interested in serving your transportation needs and in delivering prompt and reliable service on your vehicle. The best Saturn sales consultants communicate or intimate the following information:

"We don't want to sell you *one* car. After you fill up this car's odometer, we want you to be so pleased that you'll want us to sell you your *next* car."

"We want you to become an apostle for Saturn, telling friends and neighbors about your love affair with this dealership and your car."

Take a long look at these two statements. Put yourself in the place of the sales consultant from Saturn. When you discuss *your* product or service with your prospects, are you communicating these same objectives? The high-quality prospect will be intrigued and attracted.

IT'S YOUR PRODUCT, NOT YOUR PRICE

In simpler times, retailers' sales were annual or semi-annual events, usually held to make room for the upcoming season's merchandise. Today's mass marketers don't wait for a reason. The only sure-fire way to draw large numbers of shoppers to look-alike products is to have a sale. Price shoppers are poised and ready. They camp out by the mailbox and wait to grab the sales circular.

You can reach out to a different prospect. Announce new and innovative products rather than a new low price. In New England, Circuit City and Lechmere flood the airwaves with commercials announcing yet another weekend sale. By contrast, hi-fi retailer Cambridge Soundworks' current television commercial introduces a new amplified speaker system and reminds the viewer, "You can't find it anywhere else." They're applying the first Universal Law of Value—Defy Comparison—and are using their distinctive edge to attract higher quality prospects.

Red Lobster's recent television commercials help set its restaurants apart. They describe the chain's commitment to serving only the freshest fish, flown in from lakes, streams, and oceans. Unlike their previous ads, they're not promoting a sale. Prices are never mentioned. Red Lobster is announcing a distinctive, high-quality product, not a low price.

Hit the Target

Bob Pierce of Pierce Furniture in Portland, Maine, sells what he describes as a high-end product. Pierce's advertising experience has taught him that it's not just *what* you say in your advertising but *where you say it* that helps qualify customers. He was the first furniture dealer in his area to advertise on a local television station. It didn't take long for other furniture stores to follow his lead. His competitors' ads would trumpet, "Gigantic Clearance" or "Drastic Reductions." Pierce wasn't feeling drastic and refused to be lost in the 30-second shuffle. He shifted media and now advertises in the state-wide *Maine Sunday Telegram* and *Down East Magazine*.

EXHIBIT 3-1

Pierce's March Leather Sale

Everyone talks of quality but we Deliver it!

Come see all of Pierce's Leather gallery now on sale.

Sofas, Club Chairs, Wing Chairs, Recliners...and more

PIERCE
furniture

ROUNDWOOD

Design Service
Available

400 Roadwood Drive, Scarborough, ME • 207-883-1530
Pierce Furniture is off the Payne Road, just one mile south of the Maine Mall
Open Monday through Friday 9 AM to 6 PM. Thursday evenings by appointment
Saturday 9 AM to 5 PM. Sunday 12 PM to 5 PM

Pierce Furniture. Used with Permission.

Pierce works hard to ensure that his advertisements convey the high quality of his product and his manner of doing business. The low-end shopper is unlikely to be attracted to his store through the advertisement because he or she is less likely to *see* his advertisement. *Down East Magazine's* readers are upscale. Approximately one-third have a net worth between a quarter and a half million dollars. About one-quarter have earned a post graduate degree, and 40 percent own a property worth more than $150,000.

Think of your own advertising and promotional experience. Are you carefully targeting your prospects or are you a "ready, fire, aim!" type? If you have a service business, are you "cold calling" or carefully following up on qualified referrals? We've tried both methods over the past dozen years and found cold calling to be an exercise in futility. Those prospects contacted usually respond, "Steve who?," and the small number who do buy, buy only once.

Happy Customers Qualify Prospects

You can use social gatherings to attract the right kind of customers. One of our clients is a young company that provides rehabilitative services for workers who sustain on-the-job injuries. Early feedback from both patients and the patients' companies was enthusiastic. The rehab facility was anxious to grow and wondered how it could parlay these positive customer comments into new business.

We advised them to hold an after-work cookout for their own staff and for their client companies. Each client would be urged to invite a prospective client to the cookout. Doing so effectively qualifies the prospect base and provides an informal setting for satisfied customers to persuade high-quality prospects to become customers. It's adapting the effectiveness of a home-based Tupperware® party to the professional arena.

Think of ways you could gather your satisfied customers and targeted prospects. You might sponsor a local theater production and invite both clients and prospects to the performance. Perhaps you could have an outing at your local major or minor league ball park. The key is to block time either before or after the game or performance for customers and prospects to commingle. Both your customer quality and volume will increase.

PUT IT IN WRITING

Does your prospect know who you are and what you stand for? In their book *Built to Last,* James C. Collins and Jerry I. Porras explain that enduring companies like 3M,

Hewlett-Packard, Merck, and Procter & Gamble have core ideologies which reach across generations of product introductions and service innovations. Employees of these businesses are imbued with these core values, yet customers rarely are offered similar insights into the company, particularly at the prospect or premarketing stage.

Bring your mission statement out of the back hallways. Prominently display it at the entrance to your offices and in your promotional material. If the prospect understands and shares your values, you've sown seeds that can blossom into a longstanding business relationship. Like the interview process at the Saturn dealer, the prospect should discover what a customer relationship means to you and that you intend to provide continual service.

Growing numbers of customers are interested in a healthier environment, stronger communities, and effective charitable causes. Yet most customers are in the dark about the socially responsible efforts of the companies they patronize. Good news seems to arrive by accident. Consider these two examples:

While leafing through a business almanac, I spotted a list of companies that donate a high percentage of their net income to charity. Hewlett-Packard was near the top of the list. I couldn't help but wonder: "Wouldn't many customers choose an H-P product over the competition if they knew some of their dollars would be directed to the hands of the needy?"

My family made a recent trip to Kansas City and spent a Saturday morning at the Hallmark Visitors Center. My wife and I viewed an excellent film about an employee retreat for the company's artists. On our way out of the theater, we received a brochure with Hallmark's core values:

THIS IS HALLMARK

WE BELIEVE:

That our *products* and *services* must enrich people's lives and enhance their relationships.

That *creativity* and *quality*—in our concepts, products and services—are essential to our success.

That the *people* of Hallmark are our company's most valuable resource.

That distinguished *financial performance* is a must, not as an end in itself, but as a means to accomplish our broader mission.

That our *private ownership* must be preserved.

THE VALUES THAT GUIDE US ARE:

Excellence in all we do.

Ethical and moral conduct at all times and in all of our relationships.

Innovation in all areas of our business as a means of attaining and sustaining leadership.

Corporate social responsibility to Kansas City and to each community in which we operate.

These beliefs and values guide our business strategies, our corporate behavior, and our relationships with suppliers, customers, communities and each other.

Hallmark Cards Inc. Used with Permission.

Reading these values and beliefs motivated my family to do more business with our local Hallmark shop. It's unfortunate, though, that we had to travel all the way to Kansas City to discover the company's purpose. These statements of beliefs may be apparent to Hallmark employees, but are currently unknown to its retail customers. Our advice to Hallmark: Why not print all or part of your beliefs and values on that back panel of your greeting cards? We believe you'll generate repeat business for more of the right reasons.

SELLING PATIENTLY

Bob Graffy wants to create an enthusiast before he creates a customer. His stores, Cookin', the Audio & Video Specialist, Inc.™ are usually located in shopping malls, so they attract plenty of people who are just killing time while a friend, loved one, or spouse shops nearby. Some store operators think targeting people who are just killing time is a waste of time. Not Graffy's better sales representatives. They greet the visitor, offer to answer questions and when possible, wow them with a high-end audio or video system. For some, this "wowing" experience removes price as the only determinant in any future purchase decision.

"We're happy to plant the seed," says Graffy. "When the time comes that they *are* in the market, we hope that this first-time experience puts us on their shopping list." Graffy also says there's no rush. "A relationship starts to happen on a first visit, but we avoid making the prospect feel pressured."

At Action Automation & Controls, Bob Pompei also avoids rushing to sign up the new customer. In fact, he sees time as an ally. "We look for someone who's loyal to his or her existing supplier. We see it as a good sign. We're interested in the customer who doesn't fly away on a whim. Our best customers are the ones who were willing to come to us only after experiencing a series of major blunders from their earlier supplier. If we gradually persuade them to do business with us, we discover they'll be just as loyal to us." If the prospect calls and immediately asks for the price of two or three specific items, the yellow warning light begins flashing. Action's not interested in the price shopper. It's a game they won't win. "If they find a lower price next week, we know they'll drop us as quickly as they joined us," says Pompei.

REWARDING LOYALTY

If you want to sustain a high-quality customer base, it's better to invest wisely in loyal customers than spend foolishly on prospecting. MCI Preferred, a small business long-distance plan, offers a series of discounts rooted in customer devotion. If you sign an agreement saying you will retain MCI for the coming year, you save 5 percent on all long-distance calls made in that year. If you agree to remain loyal for two years, the savings are 7 percent. The customer understands that loyalty pays off more than "spinning."

Sprint has recently introduced a similar program. Stay with Sprint for a full year and you receive cash back for 10 percent of your total call volume. Sprint's advertising tag line for the program is, "It pays to stay with Sprint."

State Farm Insurance also puts its money where its loyal and safe customers are. If you have State Farm auto insurance and operate your vehicle accident-free for three years, you receive a 5 percent discount on your premiums. Drive another three years without a crackup, and you're rewarded with an additional 5 percent discount.

Here are some questions for you to consider.

1. Name a product or service that you buy strictly for the lowest price. _____

_____

2. Why is price your only consideration for this product or service? _____

_____

_____

_____

3. What's the *total cost* of *your* product or service, i.e., what are some of the benefits you offer that can justify your price, even if it's higher than your lower priced competitor?

_____

_____

_____

_____

4. Are you advertising these benefits when you promote your business?

_____

5. If no, why not? _____

_____

_____

_____

6. Track the next five customers or prospects who are interested in doing business with you. Ask each of them this question: "How did you hear about us?"

	Customer	"How did you hear about us?"
A.	_____	_____
B.	_____	_____
C.	_____	_____
D.	_____	_____
E.	_____	_____

7. Look at your list. Based on their responses, are you doing a good job of qualifying your customers?

_____

_____

8. Which response indicates the most qualified lead?

_____

_____

9. What action could you take to generate more of these leads?

_____

_____

_____

10. Do you have a mission statement for your business?

_____

11. List at least three places you'll display your mission statement so that more customers are aware of your values and beliefs.

A. _____

B. _____

C. _____

12. Where could you gather your satisfied customers and prospects to socialize (a theatrical production, ball game, cookout)? _____

_____

_____

_____

13. Who receives a better deal from your company—a *new* customer or a *loyal* customer?

_____

_____

14. What program could you introduce to reward loyalty (similar to Sprint, MCI, or State Farm Insurance)?

_____

_____

_____

_____

_____

_____

FOURTH

Narrow Your Offerings

Suppose you decide to awaken your slumbering athletic talent and join your company's lunchtime basketball league. After looking in the closet and discovering one very worn pair of canvas high tops, you decide to visit that new shoe store out on the highway.

Upon entering the premises, your lower jaw drops to the hardwood floor. This store is so big that they could hold the NCAA Final Four tournament here. Hundreds of basketball shoes are on display; 4,000 pairs of shoes are stashed behind the retail space. You look at the basketball wall and don't know where to begin. After waiting several minutes for attention that never arrives, you drift out the front door resolving to try another store with fewer shoes and more help.

A few blocks away, your cable television company announces a system rebuild and proudly proclaims that the system will soon offer over 150 channels. Immediate customer response is disappointing. "I can't keep track of the channels I have now," customers say. "Why don't they just give us good channels?"

Later that same evening, a romantic couple completes a meal in an elegant downtown restaurant and is presented with a dessert cart featuring twelve delectable

47

offerings. Each option is carefully described. But after a quick glance, they decide to hold the waist line, telling the waiter, "I think we'll pass."

The shoe store, cable television system, and restaurant have created conditions that make it easy for their customers to say "no." Displaying 200 pairs of basketball shoes doesn't add value for the customer with only two feet. One hundred and fifty channels can't be viewed by one pair of eyes. Twelve desserts bloat the decision-making process and produce a quicker request for the tab. Too many options overwhelm; selecting becomes too complicated. The transaction disappears. In this chapter, you'll discover ways to keep your product or service appealing and the sale alive.

Let's start in the shoe store. It will serve as a model for what you can do to:

- Create more value for your customer.
- Assure that *you,* not your competitor, get the sale.

STRATEGY NUMBER ONE—FUNNEL THE SHOPPER

Just for Feet sells shoes in stores like the one described in our opening example. Their typical store carries between 4,000 and 5,000 pairs of shoes. The key to their success is to simultaneously:

- offer tremendous variety and
- direct shoppers to the two or three pairs that best meet their needs.

The store offers a wide funnel of tremendous selection but narrows the funnel through expert interaction by the salesperson. For example, if your basketball shoe expedition leads you to a Just for Feet, the salesperson asks:

- **"Is there anything I can help you find today?"** If you respond "Basketball shoes," you've helped the salesperson begin to funnel the store's product offerings. A good salesperson will ask another question or two:

- **"Is there a certain brand you prefer: Nike, Reebok, New Balance?"** This question further funnels your options. You're guided from 4,000 (total shoes) to 200 (basketball shoes) to 12 (Reeboks).
- **"Do you have a budget for your purchase?"** The field is narrowed to three styles.

It's easy to say "no" when you're staring at a gymnasium-sized selection. When you're trying on three pairs, your decision undergoes a significant transformation. It's no longer *whether* to buy shoes here, it's *which* pair should I buy? The salesperson has successfully narrowed the customer's options into a choice of "yeses" and revitalized the transaction.

Just for Feet recognizes that overwhelming selection can be just that—overwhelming. That's why new store associates are taught to offer assistance near the entrance of the store before the customer begins to roam aimlessly through the store's large retail space.

Save Me Money *and* Save Me Time

Superstores are today's fastest growing segment in retailing. Books, auto parts, groceries, pet supplies, and bathroom accessories are just some of the items shoppers can now find under one massive roof. The growth is lulling many superstore owners into a sleepy mantra: "If I stock it, they will come." Sales gains will be short-lived unless they wake up and enact Just for Feet's funnel process. Most of today's customers want to save time *and* money.

Book and music superstores are among the few establishments excluded from this warning. They can offer selection with limited service because their best customers are in no hurry. A true bookworm will gladly lose himself in the shelves. Music lovers will linger around those listening stations and stereo headphones.

Everyone else has one eye on the clock. A dog owner looking for a 50-pound bag of chow for his hungry companion, or the entrepreneur in search of a toner cartridge for her office copier, has two goals: find the food (or the toner) and find the exit.

Superstore owners who trade low prices for an adequate number of "on the sales floor" personnel do so at their own peril. Tremendous selection loses its value when the poor customer feels adrift in a sea of unwanted merchandise. It's only a matter of time before the smaller store "just around the corner" experiences a revival—but only if it presents the customer with a unique selling proposition.

STRATEGY NUMBER TWO—KISS SOME FROGS

Most retailers fail to adopt a unique strategy. For example, a small shoe store in our hometown is currently shaking in its boots. MVP Sports, a sporting goods superstore, recently opened a new outlet little more than a stone's throw down the street. This week, the small store ran a newspaper advertisement announcing a basketball shoe sale with a low-price guarantee:

> If you find one of our shoes that sells elsewhere for less, we will call the other store to verify the price and upon verification, sell you the shoe for 10% less than the lowest price.

The price guarantee will sell some additional shoes, but will this store owner make any money? The advertisement sends his business straight into The Commodity Zone. In The Commodity Zone, a retailer loses his identity and becomes a clone of his lower-priced competitors. His customers enjoy lower prices, but another tack would be wiser given these facts:

- He can't stock as many shoes as the MVP Sports superstore.
- Everytime he matches a superstore price, he loses money.

Remember, MVP Sports purchases much larger quantities of each shoe and snatches a much lower price than the small store. The small store owner is being drawn to his weakness rather than playing to his strength.

Instead of saving the customer money, he could be saving the customer time. He can "kiss some frogs" for his customers. The store owner and his employees might "test drive" a wide variety of shoes offered by their suppliers and decide to sell only those few models that perform best. This permits them to confidently recommend *every* shoe that they sell. Like Just for Feet, they narrow their offerings but select quality as their calling card. A customer's shopping experience is more efficient, inspires confidence and is more likely to create repeat business.

Instead of advertising his store as the low-price leader, he can explain how his store is *different* than MVP Sports. His store is now the high-quality champion. His ad might read like this:

> You're the new general manager of an NFL team. Your goal? The Super Bowl. Will you sign everyone who shows up for team tryouts? No. Super Bowl rings land on the hands of only the very best. You want the players with great balance, lightning speed, and the will to win.
>
> At Champion Shoes, we hold tryouts with dozens of athletic shoes and cut the models that fail to make the grade. Every shoe you try on at Champion *is* a champion. Ask our salesperson for a scouting report. He or she has worn the shoe you're trying on. That's the Champion difference.

Other businesses have successfully positioned themselves as smart shoppers so their customers can be, too. John Shapiro of voice mail supplier Alliance Systems advertises his business this way:

> I first ventured into voice mail in the early '80s, during the industry's formative years, and now, 12 years later, I realize I've seen just about every bad idea that's come along. And there have been quite a few. Rapidly changing technology has created a very chaotic marketplace that's filled with new products and software and little standardization.

That's where Alliance comes in. We test and evaluate everything before we decide to stock it. If a product is not up to our standards, it never makes it to our warehouse shelves. In other words, we're picky. And we know what we're talking about. So next time you're looking for a sane voice in voice processing, give us a call. We'll throw in the advice for free.

BUYING WITH CONFIDENCE

Any business can "kiss some frogs" so customers don't have to. A neighborhood hardware store may try out 30 models of power drills and settle on selling only the 3 that perform best. If the shopper wants 30 options, she can drive down the road to Home Quarters, Builders Square, or Home Depot. She'll have more choice, maybe a lower price at the superstore, but she might end up taking home a frog rather than a prince.

A corporate meeting planner can go it alone and hope he finds a great speaker for his upcoming conference. Or he can call a high-quality speakers' bureau and rely on the bureau to narrow his purchase decision by presenting only a handful of top notch presenters from which to choose. He pays a little more, but the speakers' bureau rewards him with more time to devote to other important projects.

Mail order company Hammacher-Schlemmer features a "Best of" section in each of its catalogs. Only one model of bedside CD player or travel umbrella or bagel toaster makes the cut. The company hires consumers to test several competing brands and models and make their recommendations. These individuals "kiss some frogs," or in this case, taste some lukewarm bagels, so you won't have to.

This "kiss some frogs" concept first came to my attention in the early 1980s. My wife worked for a large corporation in Los Angeles. One of the employee perks was membership in a private store called WBS. Product offerings were similar to those of Service Merchandise or Best Buy but with only two or three choices in each product type—two or three models of stereo headphones, fax machines, and maybe two versions of pocket-sized cameras. WBS employees hand-picked the items offered for sale only after hands-on experience with each tested brand and model. This assured the purchaser that the product would meet or exceed expectations.

Many consumers will pay a premium for your knowledge and expertise. They place a value on their time. Instead of poring over *Consumer Reports* and trekking from store to store, they look for the merchant who can intelligently answer this question: "Which one do *you* think I should buy?"

For example, if a Cub Scout is about to embark on his first winter sleepover, and he needs a sleeping bag, his parents have two options:

1. Go to a sporting goods superstore, buy a reasonably priced bag, and pray for a balmy evening.
2. Visit a smaller store with fewer sleeping bags and slightly higher prices, but with salespeople who have camped out in winter temperatures.

The Keeper of Quality

The linchpin of the "kiss some frogs" strategy is the company's buyer. She must have the ability to cut through suppliers' hype and place herself squarely in the shoes of the customer: "If I were shopping in our store, would *I* want to buy this item?"

The high-quality buyer is the customer's partner. A time-pressed business executive wants to *buy* business clothing, not spend hours looking for it. She relies on the clothing store buyer's trip to the salons of New York, Dallas, Paris, or Milan. Upon the buyer's return, the salesperson can display just a handful of attractive outfits for the customer's inspection.

A hobbyist can stroll into a Brookstone store and buy with confidence. He knows the store offers a lifetime guarantee and that the items wouldn't be allowed in the store without the blessing and inspection of Brookstone's expert team of buyers.

Millions of readers choose to subscribe to *Readers Digest* or the *Utne Reader* for similar reasons. Instead of reading dozens of magazines and newspapers to keep informed, they narrow it down to one or two periodicals. In each of these cases—the clothing store, Brookstone, and the magazines—the company's buyer invests time in product selection so that the customer's time can be invested more wisely.

THE LAW OF SATURATION—THE MAGIC OF THREE

Most people find it difficult to absorb more than two or three kernels of information at a time. Speech coaches teach new speakers to present no more than three key concepts in a presentation. Jokes usually are told in threes (three horses approaching the bartender, not eight or nine). Fairy tales usually involve three characters. (How many little pigs? How many times did the big bad wolf huff and puff?) More than three kernels create information overload, or, as I call it, the Law of Saturation.

The most annoying example of this phenomenon are those "press one" telephone answering systems adopted by many large businesses. Once you're presented with your seventh or eighth option, you're ready to tear your phone out of the wall! In my first book, *How May I Help You?,* I urged businesses to limit a caller's button-pushing options to three.

Solutions for the Restaurant and Cable System

This is where the elegant restaurant makes its profit-killing mistake. Twelve dessert options make it easier to say "no." Three dessert options displayed on a tray will lead even the disciplined dieter into temptation. Dr. Donald A. Redelmeier explains a consumer's decision-making process this way: "As the number of available options increases, paradoxically the status quo becomes increasingly attractive. When a person is given only one choice, it's more tempting to go ahead and do it. If a physician gives a patient seven pieces of advice, chances are the patient will follow none of them."

What about the local cable television system? How can they simultaneously offer more channels while narrowing their offerings to make them more appealing? Hughes Satellite's DirecTV®, a cable competitor, has found a way to funnel its 175 television channels into a manageable number. Using a remote control, the viewer can ask the on-screen program guide to display narrowly defined program types—only movies or only sporting events or just news shows. For any two-hour time frame, the subscriber can consider only those programs of interest.

Here's how it works. At the bottom of the screen on the program channel, three options are displayed—movies, sports, and other. Select "movies" and the screen asks you *which* movies—drama, fantasy, musical, horror, western, comedy, and so on. Say you select musicals between 8:00 and 10:00 P.M. tonight. With a press of a button, you've transformed long and complicated listings into a personal program guide. All you see is what you want to see—musicals between 8:00 and 10:00 P.M.

Big Space, Small Selection

Warehouse clubs might intend to offer a similar strategy but are keeping the shopper in the dark. A homemaker visiting a Price Costco or a Sam's Club or a BJ's warehouse sees only three models of vacuum cleaners, but doesn't understand why. With this vast display space, couldn't they give me more options? Are these the *best* vacuum cleaners money can buy? Or, when Price Costco's buyers lowered the price bar, were these the only three manufacturers willing to do "the limbo?"

With a retail space even larger than a superstore like Just for Feet, warehouse clubs typically offer fewer product choices within each category. Here's an opportunity for one of the warehouse clubs to defy comparison and to distinguish itself in a crowded retail environment:

DEAR PRICE COSTCO SHOPPER,

We put dozens of vacuum cleaners through their paces so you wouldn't have to. Displayed here are the models that we believe to be the best value for your dollar. You can buy any of them with complete confidence.

Would this set Price Costco apart? You bet. Go to a superstore or a large discounter looking for advice on which vacuum cleaner to buy. The typical salesperson's response is: "This one's on sale."

SELLING A BETTER PRODUCT

Recent research at Stanford University indicates presenting three options might be more profitable than offering two—that offering good, better, and best increases your sales of "better." Professors Itamar Simonson and Amos Tversky presented a group of consumers with two Minolta cameras for purchase. The majority selected the less expensive of the two.

Then the professors assembled another group of consumers and added a third Minolta camera to the mix. This one was more expensive than the other two models and had correspondingly more features. "Adding the third camera caused more people in this group to choose the mid-priced camera than did in the first group." The professors conclude, "Thus, a company can steer consumers to expensive and profitable products simply by introducing more expensive ones with more features."

Honda's automobile division simplifies the buying decision by selling just three versions of its popular Accord model. Like the third camera, presenting the third and most expensive EX model draws more attention and sales to the midpriced, LX version.

Other car manufacturers have followed Honda's lead, even if by accident. In 1992, Toyota hoped to introduce mass customization of its vehicles, making it easier for customers to order their cars and trucks in any one of dozens of configurations. However, Toyota's early sales records showed that just 20 percent of the available product varieties accounted for 80 percent of the sales. Facing a weakening Japanese yen and spotting lower priced U.S. competitors on the prowl, Toyota chose to streamline its offerings exclusively to its most popular versions.

Narrowing your offerings can also lead to higher profits. It simplifies the manufacturing process, allows assembly to move in fewer straight lines, and helps the showroom close more sales. The dealer presents the prospect with fewer choices, making it easier to say "yes."

PUTTING IT TO WORK

Can you narrow your offerings? First, you'll practice on someone else. Then you'll be asked to answer some key questions about your own company.

Here are three businesses. Decide how each one can narrow its offerings and create a distinct identity in the marketplace. At the end of this chapter, I'll share my ideas on their situations.

Case Study 1: Magic Mattress

Current sales for this locally owned retailer of bedding are less than magical. National discounters flood the airwaves with great selection, low prices, and toll-free numbers. Magic Mattress offers 9 or 10 styles of mattresses in each size. They called the toll-free numbers and discovered their prices were higher than the national competitors in every size and category. What should they do?

_____

_____

_____

_____

_____

_____

_____

_____

_____

_____

_____

_____

_____

_____

_____

_____

Case Study 2: Integrity Investments

John Cartwright is a veteran employee of a large stock brokerage firm. He's ready to cut loose and be his own boss. A quick look through the yellow pages makes his entrepreneurial heart skip a beat. Over 65 investment companies are listed. To enter the fray as a me-too investor seems suicidal. How could John compete?

_____

_____

_____

_____

_____

_____

_____

_____

_____

_____

_____

_____

_____

_____

_____

_____

_____

Case Study 3: The Gold Channel

Satellite television marketers are anxious to grab a piece
of the pay television pie but recognize they're entering a
mature industry. Sales for premium cable television channels like Home Box Office and Showtime are flat. Offering
a channel with similar programming philosophy seems
doomed to failure.

To build a better product, the would-be programmers
conduct focus groups with current subscribers of the leading movie channels. Some complaints echo in each session:
"I never know when something good will be on." "Watching
HBO and Showtime is a crap shoot. Sometimes what they
show is dynamite. Other times, it's a dud." What kind of
channel should they offer?

_____

_____

_____

_____

_____

_____

_____

_____

_____

_____

_____

_____

_____

Here are some questions to consider. . .

   1. Are there any products or services that you sell that you wouldn't buy?

_____

_____

_____

_____

_____

   2. On which "narrowing" technique should you concentrate—*funneling* your offerings or *kissing some frogs?*

_____

_____

3. What product or service do you currently offer with too many options?

_____

_____

_____

4. List just two or three options/versions for that product or service.

_____

_____

_____

_____

5. List some questions you can ask your prospects that will help them funnel their selections.

_____

_____

_____

_____

_____

_____

Solution: Case Study 1

Magic decides to retire from the price wars. It starts sending home all of its mattress models with its sales department, office staff, and delivery people. They're instructed to sleep on the product and make recommendations to the owner: Which mattress produced the soundest shuteye?

Based on employee recommendations, the store cuts its model offerings and begins selling only three mattresses for each bed size: good, better, and best. Their new advertising slogan is, "Sleep on it—we do!" The salesforce uses its own experience to sell more product more enthusiastically. Dial-a-Mattress and the other national powerhouses sell more mattresses at lower prices, but Magic Mattress is delivering a unique value much closer to home.

Solution: Case Study 2

For over five years, John has tracked the burgeoning growth of socially responsible mutual funds and recognizes there's a market for this product. He chooses the name Integrity Investments for his firm because it instantly communicates his investment philosophy.

To get close to his prospects, he joins his local chapter of Businesses for Social Responsibility. He offers to make a presentation on socially responsible funds at an upcoming chapter breakfast. John also increases his community visibility by giving time to local charities, including his local United Way chapter and Habitat for Humanity. Word begins to spread about his unique product offering and business begins to grow.

Solution: Case Study 3

In order to create higher satisfaction, the programmers decide to narrow their movie offerings and schedule only those movies that earned at least one Academy Award. The schedule is anchored at 9:00 P.M., Eastern, 8:00 P.M., Central time. This predictable start time makes it easier for the time-pressed customer. The new channel also promises a high-quality program guide that will be mailed to every subscriber. The guide rates the movies on a four-star system so that the subscriber can make a more informed viewing decision.

FIFTH
UNIVERSAL LAW

Tell the Truth

Do you remember Joe Isuzu? He was that fictional, fast-talking car salesman who hosted Isuzu's television commercials in the early 1980s. Joe could make the sale, but he had this one character flaw: He lied a lot. So loose was Joe with the facts that while making his first exaggerated product claim, a simple message appeared on screen—"He's lying!"

If you want to stay ahead of the pack, tell the truth. Your customers will reward you for it. Properly executed, advertising can be a powerful way to add value to your product. All too often, advertising is a source of hyperbole undermining the advertiser's credibility and the consumer's confidence.

DANGEROUS PATH AHEAD

Two factors make advertising a high risk, high-stakes business: it's everywhere and it's not believed. Advertisers shell out serious dollars to connect with an increasingly distracted and skeptical public. Customers have reached the saturation point, discovering there's no hiding place from advertising's power. Billboards are bolted to park

63

benches, city buses, and center field fences. The grocery store is now the site of 11th hour persuasion including those little signs on your shopping cart, overhead electronic "crawl" messages, and intercom announcements.

Sports fans also get an eyeful and an earful. Today's sportscasters spend as much time hawking products as announcing the action: "The starting lineup is brought to you by Suds Beer—put Suds in *your* starting lineup. . . It's 88 degrees at game time and we're feeling a little hot under the collar up here in the broadcast booth. If *you* want to beat the heat, call Koolco, your heating and air conditioner specialist." Even baseball pitching changes have their own sponsor.

What a bunch of clutter! In her book, *Ads, TV and American Culture,* Leslie Savan estimates that the typical American reads or hears 16,000 marketing messages a day. Sixty-second commercials were once the norm. Somewhere along the way, 60-seconds was deemed too much strain on the viewers' attention span. Twice as many 30-second spots began occupying the same space. Not trusting that a viewer's attention can be held for an entire half minute, many commercials are now only 15 seconds in length. That's four times the commercials, four times as many messages competing within the same arena of attention. Breaking through, being memorable, is four times as challenging for you and your advertising agency.

And even if your message gets noticed, you're only halfway there. Consumers don't believe what's advertised. This is hardly a new phenomenon. In horse and buggy days, merchants touted magical elixirs claiming they could simultaneously cure baldness and tame rheumatism. Exaggerated claims continue to spread across the advertising landscape. Today's talk radio broadcasts are interrupted by ads for energy boosters, menopause cures, and hair restorers. Watching commercials can make you feel like a juror in a courtroom trial. You know you're hearing the truth but maybe not the whole truth—only those details the witness (advertiser) volunteers.

PENNIES FROM HEAVEN

One major credit card company's commercials showed a man holding an umbrella to protect himself from a cascading stream of cash falling from the sky. Viewers were led to believe that they'd face a similar downpour if they participated in the card's cash back program. Most cardholders barely felt a trickle. For example, a card member making $1,000 in annual purchases receives one quarter of one percent in cash back, or $2.50; not even enough to buy the umbrella.

Car commercials rarely mention the actual cost of the car. The announcer, often the dealer, announces how much you'll pay each month. What's often missing is *how many* months. Maybe you'll have to pass the loan on to your grandchildren. Print ads provide the details only in very fine print. Radio spots almost always end with the announcer breaking the speed limit with the important information about capital cost reduction payments, security deposits, interest rates, and the length of loan or lease agreement.

Unless restrained, some advertisers will commit perjury. In his book, *Where the Suckers Moon,* Randall Rothenberg provides a detailed account of car maker Subaru's quest for a new advertising campaign and agency.

In 1992, they selected Wieden & Kennedy, an Oregon-based firm best known for its compelling and off-center Nike ads. Wieden & Kennedy coveted the chance to add a carmaker to their client roster. One of the copywriters became overzealous. He was assigned the task of preparing copy for a magazine ad. Among the car's attributes, the draft copy said, were 63 safety features. Asked in an agency meeting where he got the statistic, he responded, "I made it up."

Advertising executive Alec Benn defends his industry: "Anytime anyone says, 'Advertising is a bunch of lies,' what he generally means is, 'Advertising exaggerates,' which it does—a sin the critic himself is guilty of." Advertising doesn't have to exaggerate the virtues of an added-value product or service. It can focus on a candid presentation of features and benefits. Let's examine two successful advertising campaigns that broke the mold and played it straight.

In 1959, Doyle Dane Bernbach (DDB) launched its legendary spots for the Volkswagen Beetle. DDB's work flew in the face of contemporary advertising convention. American automobiles had peaked in size, weight, and ostentation. The heavyweight champion of the era was a 1958 Buick, tipping the scales with 44 pounds of chrome.

Cars of the era were introduced on screen and in print as almost country clubs on wheels, as social icons. The ads hoped to convince the buyer that what mattered most is what your neighbors saw sitting in your driveway.

Randall Rothenberg describes what happened. "Doyle Dane proposed that Volkswagen depart from such convention by marketing itself honestly, and by using self-deprecation to impart that message. The selling proposition, the strategic foundation on which all the ads were constructed, was truthfulness."

The campaign was launched just as some American car buyers began questioning the need for tail fins and V-8 engines. Robin Fry, author of *The VW Beetle,* describes the times: "The craze for chrome and more chrome was beginning to wane, as the American motoring public began to awaken to this cripplingly expensive and highly ludicrous method of establishing their social status."

The ads struck a chord with the public because (a) they were unadorned and straightforward, and (b) they emphasized features of the car that *made it better* than their larger-sized American competitors and did so with considerable wit. Here are some examples:

- **Lemon.** This print ad features a rectangular-shaped photograph of the Beetle. The copy begins, "This Volkswagen missed the boat." It goes on to describe the exhaustive testing and inspecting of each car.

One in 50 vehicles is rejected. The ad concludes, "We pluck the lemons. You get the plums."

- **Ugly is only skin deep.** This campaign worked on many levels. It admitted the car was homely, but made the reader think about whether being "pretty" is really a critical feature for an automobile. It also helped persuade the audience that the Beetle was beautiful where it counted.

- **One of the nice things about owning it is selling it.** The ad copy describes the Beetle's excellent resale value. Advertising professionals call this a "benefit headline." You discover a benefit before you read the remaining fine print.

Exaggeration wasn't necessary. Facts were enough: 30 miles to a gallon, 40,000 miles on a set of tires, and an air cooled engine that never needed water. And unlike its larger, lovelier competitors, this car wasn't sensitive about having its photo taken. It wasn't a beauty contest. The ads were fun to read. The car was fun to drive.

BREAKING OUT OF THE COMMODITY ZONE

Doyle Dane was fortunate to have a client producing such a distinct product. Advertising becomes more challenging when you're not a beetle among giants, when you're in the middle of the pack, trapped in The Commodity Zone. Advertising agencies often send these clients off on tangents.

Beer advertising is a prime example. All major brands, save one, attempt to grab your attention with commercials packed with fast-paced humor, Funicello-like beach parties, or a combination of the two. "Oh, the beer? Yes, it tastes good. Now, back to the beach." The tag lines for these commercials can be cryptic. I drove down the expressway a few months ago and spotted a billboard for Miller Ice™: "If you get it, get it." Sorry, Miller, I don't get it—and I won't buy it.

The one exception is Heineken. Heineken may not be a better brew than Miller, Budweiser, or Coors, but it is *different*. Every two weeks, the Heineken "A-yeast" is shipped from Holland to 19 breweries around the world. Experts contend it's Heineken's yeast that sets it apart, giving the brand its distinctive taste, which beer connoisseur Michael Jackson describes as, "crisp, slightly spritzy and grassy." It's the first beer to achieve full international acceptance.

In the late 1980s, Heineken's ad agency, Warwick Baker & Fiore, created a campaign entitled, "Just being the best is enough." It focuses on product attributes, not bikinis and sight gags. One radio spot actually pokes fun at other beer ads. Three gentlemen settle on their bar stools and begin trading stories of their favorite beer commercials. "What about the one with the roller skating waitress?" One of his buddies chimes in, "Or the one with the bottle that flies through the air?" "Or how about the one with the animal that does all those tricks?" Surprisingly, their favorite beer commercials have no influence on their favorite beer. The waitress asks, "What will you guys have?" "Three Heinekens," is the immediate response.

Heineken aligns its unique recipe with a distinct style of advertising. The ads are gently paced and presented, emphasizing the tangible benefit of superior taste. The campaign reinforces the predilection of many beer drinkers—that being different is being better. *Business Week* points out, "While Heineken is an everyday brand in the Netherlands, its marketers have succeeded in transforming it into a top-shelf product almost everywhere else. In the U.S., a case of Heineken sells for twice as much as a case of Budweiser."

Both the Heineken and Volkswagen campaigns stand out for being direct, contrary to the conventions of their times, and *focusing on benefits not found in their competitors' products*. Did they tell the truth? Yes, though in Heineken's case, "being the best" is subjective.

There are enough obstacles to overcome with a wary public without misleading or exaggerating. "Besides," says advertising industry veteran Joyce DiBona, "if you make false claims, your product's not going to last long."

BEYOND ADVERTISING—PUBLIC RELATIONS

Advertising alone won't sell your wares. Remember that of all the possible methods available to communicate your message, advertising credibility is probably the most suspect. The audience recognizes that the time and space is paid for by a less-than-objective communicator. That's why most successful businesses use a multifaceted approach to create product awareness.

Skillful public relations campaigns can generate news stories more easily accepted and believed than commercials. Favorable press affects your marketplace stature and can increase your product sales. Charity work and community service are effective ways for fledgling enterprises to make themselves known.

Ken Kragen is the personal manager of many of today's top show business stars. He teaches his clients to see advertising as just one item in the toolbox used to build awareness. In his book, *Life Is a Contact Sport,* Kragen recommends a full-court press approach to promotion: advertise, make yourself available to the media, and give back through charitable contributions and performances. In 1985, he persuaded many of his clients to participate in fundraising efforts for the victims of famine in Central Africa. The musical fruit of his labor, the recording of "We Are the World," became an international anthem, raising awareness and needed funds for the less fortunate. This work of charity benefitted millions of hungry families while showing the tender side of his talented clients.

Kragen says that good deeds are good business. At the core of his managing style is the event strategy. To reach the next level of success in any business, Kragen argues, develop multiple media exposures within a relatively short period of time. He used this method in 1993 to boost the career of country singer Travis Tritt.

In late 1992, Tritt's album was nominated for a Grammy Award. That's when Kragen went to work. He persuaded CBS to let Tritt make a guest appearance on the awards show. He also talked the network into moving up the airing of a Tritt-featured TV movie, *Rio Diablo,* to the following Sunday. Tritt had also just completed filming a commercial for Budweiser. The commercial wasn't scheduled to air for another month. With all of these other Tritt exposures, Budweiser asked the obvious question: "Why wait?" All of these appearances, plus a guest spot on *The Tonight Show,* occurred inside of one week.

In a meeting with movie studio executives, casting directors and producers, Tritt heard, "Everywhere I look this week, I see you. Congratulations on all of your success." Multiple exposure creates those comments.

ADVERTISING THAT'S NOT FOR SALE

Your advertising is a source of information that reaches both the willing and the skeptical. But there's another source of information beyond reproach—your customers. Word-of-mouth is the single most effective weapon in the never-ending battle for market share. You can't buy it. You can't borrow it. You must earn it. People don't talk about mediocre products, only those that are outstanding or disappointing.

Nothing kills a bad product faster than good advertising. Strong advertising motivates consumers to try a new product. Then the most credible advertising, word-of-mouth, takes over. Early samplers warn the undecided to save their money.

Movie marketers recognize that bad movies (the duds) benefit the most from good advertising. Good movies (the gems) benefit most from word-of-mouth. The marketing plan for a movie that studios know is a dud is:

1. Run lots of ads *before* the film opens.
2. Open the film on a weekend on as many screens as possible.
3. Avoid preview screenings so that early reviews can't sour potential viewers.
4. Collect lots of money at the ticket booth and pray that people don't ask for their money back.

By Monday, word-of-mouth begins to spread through the breakfast counters and around the water coolers. By the following weekend, the theater's almost empty. The movie studio hurriedly makes plans for the dud's release on video.

Studios confident that they're releasing a gem need not be obsessed with total saturation on the opening weekend. What's important is that *some* people see it. Word-of-mouth then permeates through the masses more thoroughly than all of the billboards, commercials, and radio spots the studio might produce. Each weekend's ticket sales exceed the previous weekend's tally. The gem enjoys an extended stay in the theater and the studio anticipates a profitable release in the video store.

> The fastest way to grow your business:
> Speak about your product or service the same way your customers do.

Word-of-Mouth in Advertising

Buena Vista Pictures, a division of The Walt Disney Co., cleverly uses word-of-mouth to promote its very best films. When the studio's confident a film will play well, it's advertised and released on a special, one-night sneak preview. Word quickly spreads from the first-night audience to potential

ticket buyers. *Mr. Holland's Opus,* starring Richard Drey-
fuss, was introduced in this fashion and enjoyed a strong
box office run in early 1996.

The film and theater industry have devised another
way to use word-of-mouth in their advertising campaigns.
When is a customer most enthusiastic about a great play
or movie? On the way out the theater's door. Commercials
show movie or theatergoers emptying out of special screenings, and cameras capture their enthusiastic comments.
The viewer at home is getting a recommendation from the
most trusted source, the customer.

Viking Office Products delivered word-of-mouth in the
pages of its most recent product catalog. On page 5, customer Samuel R. Finglass of Royal Palm Beach, Florida,
communicates a tangible benefit:

> On the afternoon of June 19th, I phoned an order to your
> Jacksonville branch and the next day, the order was at my
> door. Instead of driving to our local office supply store, in
> all kinds of weather and traffic . . . park[ing] my car,
> walk[ing] into the store, finding the right merchandise,
> then waiting at the cashier line to pay and then driving
> back to my office, takes approximately 2 hours of my time.
> It takes 5 minutes to order the same merchandise by
> phone, saving time, money and no delivery cost.

PRIMING THE PUMP

Like the movie studio or the office supplier, your first and
most important task is to offer a product or service so consistently good and so distinctive it's worthy of glowing
word-of-mouth. But delivering an outstanding product
isn't always good enough. Good word-of-mouth travels at
its own pace. Let's say two business associates, one of
whom is your customer, meet at the gym. Will your name
come up? A telephone conversation is conducted between
one of your delighted customers and a prospect. Will your
product be a part of the conversation?

Waiting for word-of-mouth can make you feel like the Maytag repairman. It's a long time between calls. Smart businesses sow the seeds of conversation, finding ways to accelerate the good news. "Priming the pump" makes the phone and the cash register ring.

Amica Mutual Insurance is the master of word-of-mouth. Amica does no consumer advertising in established markets, relying solely on positive word-of-mouth from their existing policyholders. These over-the-backyard-fence conversations are fueled by the outstanding service provided by Amica's employees.

Twice a year, Amica helps satisfied customers strike up the conversation. Each policyholder receives a copy of Amica's annual report, and many of them receive a card requesting the names and addresses of friends who could benefit from Amica. Later in the year, they receive a Thanksgiving card. Inside the card is another request for the names of friends. Although the primary purpose is to show appreciation to its policyholders, Charles Horne, an Amica senior vice president, points out, "We generate so much new business from the Thanksgiving mailing that the mailing more than pays for itself."

The company is currently testing a third mailing to selected policyholders called a "pass along package." Inside the envelope, the policyholder finds:

- A letter explaining how referrals benefit him or her: ". . . by referring others to Amica, you also help your company grow. And continued growth ensures a strong financial base, which is your guarantee of protection in good times and bad."
- A brochure designed for the friend, "Discovering the Meaning of Amica."
- An Auto Rate Quotation Request Form.

Amica hopes that policyholders will either pass it along immediately or will save it for the "just right" moment when the conversation turns to insurance.

"Just right" moments can be the key to spreading word-of-mouth. Customers are most likely to talk about you when they are most pleased with you. Amica seizes such opportunities. Claim settlements often arrive sooner than the policyholders expect. Guess what occasionally arrives *with* the settlement check? A referral card. Amica typically returns 20 percent of its auto premium annually in a dividend check. What better time to ask for names of interested friends, co-workers, and neighbors than when this unexpected check arrives in the mailbox?

Amica's experience dispels the notion that you have to pay customers for referrals. These referring policyholders are compensated only in knowing that their friends or family members will be happy with the switch.

Though not a corporate mandate, conscientious Amica agents write letters of thanks to each policyholder who makes a referral that leads to an inquiry or new business. Such follow-up pays the company dividends. Mr. Horne points out, "We have some policyholders so sold on us that they don't wait for referral cards. They call us up and tell us who we should be calling. These loyal customers are crusaders on our behalf."

Scott Cook uses another name for his secret salesforce—"apostles." Cook is the founder of Intuit, maker of Quicken® financial software. Here's what his company's operating values statement says about word-of-mouth:

> It means giving customers dramatically more value than they expect—whether measured by price, performance, quality, features, or service. We know we're succeeding when we inspire customers to go out and tell others about our company.

It's working. Most people try Quicken because of an enthusiastic recommendation from a friend, family member, or business associate.

Inspire? Crusaders? Apostles? This is starting to sound like a tent revival. Word-of-mouth may not be spiritual, but it sure is emotional. Customers sell you when they're excited about what you've sold them. No one sells you better. Just look at Amica and Intuit:

- Intuit's Quicken® is used by over 10 million people. Until 1989, Intuit had only two salespeople on its staff.
- Amica Mutual has nearly half a million policyholders. It has *no* full-time salespeople.

Intuit has considered ways to speed up the word-of-mouth process because as Intuit group marketing manager Suzanne Taylor reports, "We know that word-of-mouth is a critical factor in why people buy our product. But the idea of providing a financial incentive, that is, putting customers on commission, fell flat on its face.

"When asked about the possibility," Taylor continues, "customer response was overwhelmingly negative. We discovered in research that customers derive intrinsic satisfaction in telling someone about a product they really believe in and benefit from. Our customers didn't want family members or friends thinking they were recommending the product for the money." The experience of Amica and Intuit suggests that if your product is exceptional, you need not pay for word-of-mouth; in fact, paying for referrals might taint the process.

My own speaking and training business relies heavily on word-of-mouth:

- My name, address, and phone number is on *every* page of printed material that our clients receive. Every handout page, case study, and follow-up mailing acts like a business card. We make it easy for a client to pass our name along.
- Every seminar attendee is asked to evaluate the program. At the bottom of the form is the phrase, "Steve, I'll recommend your services to the following individual." Space is provided for the prospect's name, address, phone number, and the name of the attendee providing the referral.

Find ways to put your satisfied customers (your apostles) *and* your prospects in the same place at the same time. As mentioned in "Qualify Your Customers," we recommend to our clients that they have an evening cookout and invite their best salespeople (their customers) to socialize with their best prospects. Word-of-mouth will do the rest.

Gathering only your customers for a good time can also fuel word-of-mouth. In the summer of 1994, 40,000 loyal owners of Saturn automobiles descended on Spring Hill, Tennessee, for the first-ever cookout and rally. The event received generous national publicity and undoubtedly triggered plenty of Saturn-related conversations by participants when they returned home.

Here are some other important questions to answer:

1. Think about your current efforts to advertise your business. Are you communicating those features that make your product distinct and unique?

_____

_____

_____

_____

2. How could you include *your customers* in your advertising?

_____

_____

_____

_____

3. What features haven't you been promoting that you should be?

_____

_____

_____

_____

4. If good news is spreading about you, how can you _accelerate_ your word-of-mouth? (Could you send a "pass-along" package to your satisfied customers? Could you ask for referrals where you collect evaluation forms or comment cards? Could you send greeting cards on a holiday when no one else does and include a postcard asking for referrals?)

_____

_____

_____

_____

_____

_____

5. Look beyond advertising for other ways to promote your business. What are you doing that's newsworthy? What's so unusual or unique about your business that people would like to read or hear about?

_____

_____

_____

_____

6. What charity could use your help? Do you have a
skill that you could donate?*

_____

_____

_____

_____

_____

_____

---

* You could make publicizing your contribution a top priority, but doing so
misses the point. Focus on the cause, not the effect, trusting that the effect
will take care of itself. Three years ago, local businessman Bob Pierce
called us at Christmas asking for a year-end contribution to the Salvation
Army. At no point in the conversation did he mention that he owned
Pierce Furniture. We were so impressed with his humble approach that
within six months we were in his store buying a new couch.

SIXTH
UNIVERSAL LAW

Consistency Beats Occasional Excellence

"Knock their socks off!" "Dazzle, delight, and wow 'em!" "Create Raving Fans." It's the advice you're offered while browsing through the customer service section of your bookstore. It's also enough to make you feel inadequate. Your customers don't expect to be "wowed" or "delighted"; just deliver the same quality every time.

When we eat spaghetti in our house, we don't anticipate a "delightful" experience with the sauce. We choose Ragu. Ragu isn't as good as the sauce at the local Italian restaurant, but here's the reason we buy it: It tastes the same every time. Like most customers, we seek the predictable and reliable.

CREATING DÉJÀ VU

Best Western used to advertise that no two of its hotels were alike. The advertising campaign was short-lived, for good reason. Most travelers seek out hotels that *are* alike. Why open the door and get surprised? One of Best Western's competitors uses its pocket directory to rate each of its properties on a one-to-five scale. Would you check into a hotel with one lonely little star next to its name?

By contrast, Red Roof Inns takes pride in across-the-board identical rankings. All of the inns are company owned, rather than held by franchisees. Every location operates at the same standards. Turn the key, open the door, and you'd swear you've stayed in this room before.

Red Roof Inns have special appeal for the frequent traveler who simply wants a good night's sleep. There are no fancy lobbies and no on-site restaurants. What you get is a bed with a high-quality mattress and a television set with reception that makes you feel like you're home.

At least twice a year, Red Roof's audit team descends upon each site to conduct a thorough inspection of housekeeping, maintenance, and the hotel's financials. Everyone from the chain's chief operating officer to the location's manager receives a report. Any shortcomings or deviations from standard operating procedure are quickly corrected.

Fifteen years ago, Red Roof urged travelers to "Sleep Cheap™." Today, inexpensive sleeping options are all over the road. Red Roof now highlights a more unique and attractive product attribute: no surprises. Consistency beats occasional excellence.

Those Arches Are *Always* Golden

Fast food restaurants were open for business long before Ray Kroc dreamed of bringing McDonald's to your neighborhood. In the 1920s, Roy Allen and Frank Wright used their distinctive root beer to create the first franchised chain. A & W asked each franchisee for $2,000 per location and supplied all restaurateurs with identical root beer syrup and cooling equipment. But there was a missing piece in their fast food puzzle—across-the-board consistency. The chain had hundreds of outlets but, outside of the root beer syrup, there was little uniformity in their menu and operations.

In the early 1950s, the original McDonald brothers sought to expand the McDonald's experience beyond their original San Bernardino, California location. Like Allen and Wright, they overlooked the missing piece. According to John L. Love, in *McDonald's: Behind the Arches:*

> Franchisees were buying only the blueprints to a red-and-white-tile building, the right to use the arches, a fifteen page operating manual . . . and the McDonald's name . . . After that, they were free to operate as they wished, and most did. They sold their hamburgers at different prices. Some added new items to the menu. Others added more serving windows. One licensee even decided to bring the golden arches to a point and rename his drive-in. He called it Peaks . . . Not surprisingly, sales at the franchised stores did not begin to approach those at the brothers' drive-in."

Franchisees weren't satisfied following instructions. They wanted to tinker. To grow more predictably and successfully, you can:

- take a centrally-owned Red Roof Inns approach or . . .
- create a franchising system that guarantees consistency throughout the chain.

Ray Kroc chose the latter. John F. Love says:

> While other chains started out permitting franchisees to deviate, conformity to operating standards was bedrock principle to Kroc from the beginning . . . McDonald's took more seriously the task of building a uniform operating system. That created a difference where there had been none. McDonald's franchisees could be counted on to deliver the same quality of food and service time after time, restaurant after restaurant. Its competitors, by their own admission, did not duplicate that.

FAMILIARITY BREEDS PROFITS

A consistent product or service makes the customer's purchase decision a *fait accompli*. Imagine the vacationing family driving down the road and hearing hungry pleas from the back seat. Two restaurants appear on the horizon—a McDonald's and a Charlie's Grill. Charlie's has 19-cent hamburgers. But which restaurant gets the order? The one with the Happy Meals™. A traveling salesperson has a choice in overnight accommodations— Red Roof Inn or Charlie's Motor Lodge. The salesperson knows that this Red Roof will be no different than the last Red Roof. She knows nothing about Charlie except for his room rates. Maybe he's a better cook than innkeeper. Most customers will pay a fair and profitable price for the predictable.

Take Yourself Out to the Ballgame—What You'll Learn

Some industries have learned how to deliver a consistently satisfying experience even with a product of uneven quality. Your local sports team is a case in point. A three-run homer may win the game for the home team. Pandemonium erupts in the stands. Everyone goes home happy. But just as likely, the visiting team will compile a double-digit lead by the seventh inning stretch. No one feels like rooting for the home team, right?

True, but today's contests might make you forget there's a scoreboard. Rock music plays between innings or during changes of possession. The clock occasionally stops, but there's no such thing as a time out. Expect playful high jinks between the team's mascot and the officials, or a Rockette-like dance routine from the local cheerleaders. Or watch kids running the bases, or shooting hockey pucks, or throwing footballs to win trips to Disney World. The outcome of the game is hard to call but there's one sure bet—the energy, noise, laughter, and cheering will be the same whether the home team plays like the 1929 Yankees or the 1962 Mets.

CONSISTENCY IN TANGIBLES

The Total Quality Management (TQM) movement swept through international assembly lines during the 1980s. "That's good enough" was no longer enough. "Zero defects" became the battle cry. Consumers were treated to more consistently built products in every conceivable category; better cars, computers, and candy bars. At Hershey Foods, building identical candy bars is a religion. A Hershey's® Milk Chocolate with Almonds chocolate bar is 1.45 ounces—not 1.4 ounces, but 1.45 ounces. Why should the next or last person in line get any more or any less?

This slavish attention to product consistency helps Hershey Foods stay out of The Commodity Zone. Branded items like Hershey's® bars don't escape the discount bin because they're "fabulously great." It's because they're always good. Hershey's and other well-known brands command a full price because of:

- **A historical track record.** Today's purchase results from yesterday's satisfactory consumption or outcome.

- **Modern-day delivery of consistency.** Consistent production practices and quality control keep the guesswork out of the purchase decision.

So how about *you?* Are you always selling the equivalent of a Hershey's bar? Or is your product or service occasionally more like an empty wrapper? There's no mystery in living by the Law of Consistency. It requires a single-minded commitment to sameness. The companies that create loyalty deliver consistency. Why do more than half of Toyota's customers return to Toyota showrooms for their next car? They hate surprises. Unlike its competitors' claims, a Toyota Corolla™ does not build excitement or create a passion for the road. Its owners love the car's most outstanding standard feature. It starts.

INCONSISTENCY IN INTANGIBLES

Unfortunately, a parallel revolution isn't taking place in service industries. People aren't performing as consistently as machines. For example, the hospital patients I interview rarely comment on the precision-built equipment used to diagnose or alleviate their conditions. They want to talk about people—the nurse who held their hand while a multimillion dollar diagnostic imager rumbled around them; or, by contrast, the nurse on the overnight shift who ignored their 3:00 A.M. pleas through the patient call button.

What's true for spaghetti sauce, candy bars, cars, and fast food restaurants is true for hospitals and all other service businesses. The customer doesn't demand a service all-star, just someone who's a solid performer.

TQM's lack of influence on the intangibles is evident each time I prepare to train for my clients. One of my recent seminars was for a chain of hardware stores. One Saturday morning, I watched a customer approach the counter and ask, "Is Paulette working today?" The clerk responded, "No, she won't be back in until Tuesday. Is there something I can help you with?" The customer simply said, "No, I'll come back."

BUILDING CONSISTENCY

There are steps you can take to deliver a more consistent purchase experience.

Hire Right

Insist on hiring people who have previously demonstrated a desire to serve. Always check references, and always trust your instincts. It only takes one sourpuss to sabotage your efforts to deliver quality service. You want the customer who asks for Paulette to discover that *everyone* working in the store is a Paulette. If you interview your customers and discover that they're always satisfied with the service received, take it as a compliment.

Grow Slow

Grow at a pace commensurate with your ability to find high-quality people. Portmanteau, based in Portland,

Maine, hand-produces distinctive canvas handbags and luggage. Owner Nancy Lawrence refuses to transform her artisan workshop into a more efficient and larger-scale assembly line. She and her two full-time employees take pride in shepherding each piece from the initial creative cloudburst to a finished product. Lawrence knows she could be growing faster, but the growth would require she become a full-time manager and abandon her first love, sewing.

Her choice of "doing" over "managing" guarantees that her business delivers a consistently durable and attractive product. Faster production would accelerate sales, but consistency of product would become uneven. Just one poorly made item could engender negative word-of-mouth.

Successful consultants face a similar decision. They can either grow to meet demand or stay a one-person shop to limit supply. Choosing to stay small creates a pivotal selling point: "When you buy me, you get me." Consistency of the service delivered is easier to control. At the faster growing firm, customer satisfaction is directly linked to the quality of the assistant or associate handling the project. Every task performed in a mediocre fashion affects the reputation and the value of the name on the door. In the case where the owner is the brand, the brand itself is diluted by uneven efforts and results.

Personalize the Contact

Marcam™ Corporation of Newton, Massachusetts, sells highly sophisticated, technical software to process manufacturers; i.e., products formed from the blending of ingredients. Marcam's technical support is critically important to those manufacturers relying on the information the software provides. Marcam surveyed its veteran customers and asked what could be done to improve its technical support. One of the most frequent responses was: "I want to talk to someone who knows my company and understands how we apply the software." In other words, the customer wants to avoid a "spin the wheel and take your chance" approach and instead be able to bet on a "sure thing."

Marcam responded by dividing its technical specialists into six self-directed work teams. Each customer is routed to his or her own work team. Support specialist contact is narrowed, and they now field more calls from fewer customers and become more familiar with the client's application strategies and manufacturing process.

Think of ways you can "pair up" your customer with one (or just a handful) of your employees. Many insurance agencies assign a new customer to a specific customer service representative. Hospital patients tell me they prefer seeing the same nurse or nurse's aide each shift throughout a stay. Creating a relationship between customer and employee increases the likelihood of consistently high-quality service and that the customer will come back.

Introduce One Skill at a Time

Let your newly hired employees face only the situations they're ready to handle. Prioritize all of the skills you want them to master and teach the skills in that order. Don't expect total mastery by the time they collect their first paycheck; you can ensure consistent service by mastering one skill at a time.

Each week, thousands of personal computer users toss out their old checkbook registers and replace them with Intuit's Quicken® on their PCs. These thousands of new customers spawn hundreds of new questions directed to Intuit's Albuquerque, New Mexico, technical center. New technical support representatives are hired continuously. Fast growth threatens the consistent outcome of service quality. Scott Faulds, group supervisor of Intuit's personal financial group, shares these techniques, which help assure a predictably satisfactory response:

•**Train Before the Trenches.** No one is rushed into battle. As Faulds puts it, "We don't throw people into the deep end of the pool." Each new technical support representative spends at least four weeks in training before being isolated on the phone with querulous customers. During part of this training period, they watch experienced reps field live customer calls.

- **Skill-based Routing.** Unlike most call centers, calls at Intuit are not sent to "the next available representative." They're routed by product type. Here's how it works. The Quicken 5 for Windows users' manual lists a different technical support phone number than the manual for a product like Quick-Pay™ or ExpensAble™ for Windows. Calls for ExpensAble are sent to reps well-versed in ExpensAble. Confused Quicken 5 users are routed to confident Quicken 5 support reps. This call-routing method allows Intuit to train new reps on a limited number of specific products or what they call "skill sets." The new reps builds confidence because all of their incoming calls are limited to products they know. Just as importantly, customers feel confident that they are receiving accurate information and useful help.

As you grow your business, make your highest priority the delivery of a consistent, high-quality product or service. Consistency instills customer confidence. Confident customers don't waste time considering alternatives. They take the shortest route to satisfaction—through *your* door.

Here are some questions to answer. . .

1. Is your product or service as consistent as it could be? If no, why not?

  _____

  _____

  _____

  _____

2. What specific steps can you take to ensure you're delivering a consistent product or service?

_____

_____

_____

_____

_____

3. Think about Hershey's chocolate bars and Portmanteau's handmade canvas luggage. Which product more closely resembles yours? Should you be emulating the assembly line or the artisan's workshop?

_____

_____

_____

_____

_____

_____

SEVENTH

Keep in Touch (More than a Bill)

Go to the mailbox today and see what your postal carrier deposited. You probably heard from one or two companies. Let me guess—they wrote you notes that say, "Thank you for shopping with us. We know you had a choice and we appreciate your continued patronage." What, you're not receiving these love notes? Maybe your correspondence sounds more like this: "Give us your money."

Most companies work hard to get new business and ignore old business. Prospects get wined and dined. Loyal customers do the dishes. An unappreciated customer develops a roving eye and is either tempted by competitive offers or simply gives up on the relationship.

DEAR JOHN . . .

One year ago, I decided to cancel my American Express Gold Card membership. Seventy five dollars a year seemed too much to pay when competitors flooded my mailbox with no-fee offers. Until the time I called to cancel, I heard from American Express exactly 12 times a year—they sent me a bill. Wow, did the level of attention change once I said, "I don't love you anymore." The final bill included a message to the effect, "We miss you. Please reconsider." Sorry, American Express. Where was all this care and concern before we broke up?

As it turned out, American Express *did* win me back. They offered me a $50 credit towards a meal at a restaurant of my choice. I accepted. Since our initial break-up, the company has made great strides in applying the Seventh Universal Law: Keep in Touch.

If you want to avoid "Dear John" letters from your customers, live this piece of advice: Pay more attention to the customers you have than to the customers you want. You'll discover that "we love you" works much better than "we miss you." And it doesn't have to cost an arm and a leg to show your appreciation. Our local People's Heritage Bank displays this sign at the entrance:

> "Welcome,
> Whether you've been with us for years or just opened your first account . . . Thanks for your business."

The sign is a silent but continual reminder that the customer made a wise decision.

When we moved into our new home two years ago, *Sports Illustrated* saw an opportunity to keep in touch. I received a postcard with a picture of a baseball player sliding under a catcher's tag. It said, "From now on your *Sports Illustrated* will be crossing a new home plate—how does it feel?" I opened the flap and read, "Just wanted to join the crowd welcoming you to your new home. Here's wishing you all the best now and in the future."

> **Pay more attention to the customers you have than to the customers you want.**

The reason this gesture was so effective was because there *wasn't* a crowd welcoming us to our new home. Only one company used our change of address request to create a customer contact *outside* of the billing envelope.

Your customers are constantly being courted by the other guy. Smart companies neutralize competitors and maintain *market share in the mind* through well-timed mailings, special offers, or loyalty rewards.

CREATING A LONG MEMORY

When you buy a new car, the chances are you'll get a phone call from the salesperson within 30 days asking, "How's the car running? Are there any questions I can answer for you?" After 30 days, you're disconnected. Car dealers that prosper find a better way. Almost 10 years ago, we leased a car through Charles River Saab in Watertown, Massachusetts. We *still* receive the seasonally published *Charles River Saab Review*. Their persistence may seem a bit overzealous. But for some lapsed customer, that newsletter falls on the doorstep on the very day the recipient was planning to visit a car showroom.

One of your company's least appreciated assets is its mailing list:

- Feed it and make it grow.
- Collect a name and address each time a customer does business with you.
- Capture the name and address of anyone who inquires about you. Maybe they're not ready to buy, but they'll never be back unless you have a way to occasionally dangle your name in front of them.

The list of creative ways to keep in touch is endless. Here are the most commonly used methods:

Newsletters

You can produce a great publication inexpensively and reach everyone on your list simultaneously. The most attention-grabbing newsletters are *visual;* they go easy on the words, because there's so much else your customer *has* to read. Use *humor;* your piece will move to the top of the mail pile if you've made your customers laugh in past issues. Cartoons are a great use of space. Be *informative:* remember, your customers would rather read about your people than your products or services.

Go easy on the selling. It's called a *news*letter for a reason. Felix Bosshard at Charles River Saab discusses news about products, but he also weighs in on important topics like the health of his grandchildren and the upcoming season of the Boston Classical Orchestra—in his words, "my favorite cultural organization."

Greeting Cards

Newsletters help you reach all of your customers at once. But a greeting card can help you connect with one customer at a time. The best occasion to remember? The day every other business forgets—your customer's birthday. Every September 23, Delta Airlines' Dusty the Air Lion™ sends our son, Kevin, a birthday card. It makes an impression on him but also on his airline-ticket-buying parents. When you sign up new customers, ask for their birthday and use it once a year to spread good cheer.

Phone Calls

This may be a better way than a greeting card to reach someone during the December holidays. Plenty of companies send a seasonal card; few take the time to pick up the phone. Phone calls are a great way to let lapsing customers know about a special or a new product introduction. MCI occasionally calls existing customers with a unique twist. Instead of discussing ways to spend more money, they explore ways the customer could *save* money on their long distance bill. Do you call your customers to announce new locations, upcoming sales, or other good news? Make sure you have a specific reason for the call. It will make the contact more relaxed and effective.

Affinity Program Statements

This innovative way to keep in touch took off on May 1, 1981, when American Airlines introduced its Advantage™ program. Every mile flown on American was tallied, accumulated, and made redeemable for American travel awards. American's trailblazing concept has been widely copied throughout the travel and credit card industries. Maybe you should copy it, too. The monthly or quarterly statement posting points, miles, or dollars is a "good news" letter. It's the direct opposite of a bill. Instead of stating, "Here's what you owe *us* . . .," you're announcing, "Here's what we owe *you* . . ."

Plenty of businesses stay competitive by rewarding the loyal customer. Your morning coffee mug might have the name of the coffee shop emblazoned on the side. The mug merits a discounted refill. Some coffee shops stamp your frequent drinker card and reward you with your 11th cup free.

If you introduce a similar program, make it hasslefree. Your customers have enough little slabs of plastic and paper in their wallets. Don't make them carry any more. Create a program in which you track the customer through your point-of-purchase terminal.

Catalogs

Your catalog is another excellent way to say, "Remember me?" Consider printing a note or letter in each issue. Portmanteau owner Nancy Lawrence discovered that customers pay close attention to the correspondence. In a recent catalog, she personally signed a letter to customers. They responded by calling to place orders and insisting on speaking to Nancy—only Nancy! The most recent catalog also features a letter, but this one reduces the bottleneck. It's signed, "Your friends at Portmanteau."

Personalized Letters

You can use a word processing program's mail merge feature to create personal letters to both loyal and lapsed customers. Max Grassfield of Grassfield's Men Store in Denver uses this type of correspondence as part of his Invitational Marketing™ program. Loyal customers receive a personal invitation to upcoming Grassfield sales events. Each letter contains a personal salutation and is signed by an individual salesperson. The results have been similar to those witnessed by Nancy Lawrence at Portmanteau. A one-to-one relationship is developed or rekindled.

Viking Office products uses a personal letter to bring straying customers back into the fold. The one we received is reproduced in Exhibit 7-1. Viking also enclosed a postage-paid envelope for our response.

Max Grassfield composed a similar letter that his salespeople mail to customers who haven't visited his store in over a year:

Dear Dusty:

I was catching up with some of my customers the other day when it occurred to me that I haven't seen you in the store for some time. I hope you're well and life is treating you kindly.

Next time you're in Cherry Creek North, why don't you drop by? It would be great to get caught up with you and I could show you some of our new arrivals. We have some wonderful items this season that I think you would really like.

Look forward to seeing you.

Rick McGowen

P. S. Max told me to tell you that through October 30th, he'll give you $25 off your first $100 purchase. What a guy!

E X H I B I T   7 – 1

10/20/95   Customer #123456

Steve Broydrick
Steve Broydrick Associates
P.O. Box 7240
Portland, ME 04112

Dear Steve Broydrick:

THIS HALF IS OURS:	**THIS HALF IS YOURS:**

THIS HALF IS OURS:

We haven't heard from you since
your last order for office supplies
a few months ago.

That bothers me.

Losing a good customer is like
losing a good friend. I can't
let either drift away in silence.

If we're at fault, I'd like to
know, and make it right.
Whatever the reason, I do care.

The other side of this "Half"
letter is yours. I'd consider
it a personal favor if you'd
use it.

Sincerely,

VIKING OFFICE PRODUCTS

Irwin Helford
President

IH: cjw

879 W. 190TH STREET • P.O. BOX 61144 • LOS ANGELES, CA 90061–1000
(310)225-4500 • FAX: (310)327-2376

When you change your address or phone number, you can notify everyone on your mailing list with a personalized letter. It's a snap using mail merge.

BE HARD TO FORGET

Personalized letters can also be used to remind your customers or prospects what you've done for them. Many executive search firms create and mail quarterly newsletters. Boston-based Kiradjieff & Goode always finishes up a successful search with a letter to everyone who was contacted during the process. The letter is used to meet two objectives:

1. To offer thanks in helping complete the successful search.
2. To sell the benefits of doing business with Kiradjieff & Goode in the future.

The letter details the number of candidates Kiradjieff & Goode screened for their clients. They remind the contact that they practice the Fourth Universal Law—Narrow Your Offerings: "By screening fourteen individuals for every candidate we presented to [name of clients] we ensured they met only the most qualified and motivated professionals who fit superbly within their organization."

The company also reminds its contacts, "Kiradjieff & Goode is passionately committed to our engagements." The firm's six executive search professionals range in age from 33 to 59. The staff is a diverse blend of skills and backgrounds. "This enables us to attract top performers at all levels of experience."

This is a strategy worth emulating. You become more valuable when you (a) "deliver the goods," and then (b) remind your customer that you delivered the goods.

Customer Appreciation Parties

Had a good year? Why not share your good fortune with those who made it possible? Invite *everyone*—your customers, vendors, even your prospects to a reception at your place of business. Send invitations to customers *everywhere*. There's nothing wrong with long distance no-shows. The invitation's your way of saying, "I'm thinking of you."

Mail Questionnaires

Asking for feedback is another way to stay on your customer's mind. Make sure you request a reasonable amount of your customer's time. Today's savvy organizations are streamlining their questionnaires and realizing a higher return rate.

Specialty Advertising

A useful premium item helps your customer remember you and develop amnesia toward your competitors. What items do you keep in your work area: Sticky notes? A mouse pad? A calendar? Ask your friends and colleagues what items they appreciate and contact a high-quality provider. Remember, the quality and durability of the item reflects the quality of your business.

Here are three other innovative ways to keep in touch:

- **Rebate checks.** When you sell a product, you create a single customer contact; if you mail a rebate check, you produce an echo. The customer might have forgotten he completed the coupon and is pleasantly surprised by the cash and the attention.

> By the way, do you *keep* the name and address of that customer? It's better than sending mail to "Occupant."

- **Signs at the exit.** Customers tend to remember the last words they see or hear during contact or visit. "Thank you for your business" creates a positive last impression. Some computer software companies program a "thank you" into their application. They display their appreciation everytime the customer chooses to exit.
- **30-Day Postcards.** We send postcards with three key ideas from our seminars to every attendee on the one-month anniversary of the program. You can create a similar lasting impression. Write a note or postcard to every new customer within 30 days of their first purchase, thanking them for their business.

Here are some questions to answer.

1. Have you ever stopped doing business with a company because you felt forgotten or unappreciated?

   _____

   _____

2. What techniques could that company have used to keep in touch?

   _____

   _____

   _____

   _____

   _____

3. List all of the ways you currently keep in touch with your customers (a bill doesn't count!).

   _____

   _____

   _____

   _____

_____

_____

_____

_____

4. A prospect calls and inquires about your product or service. You offer to mail him a brochure or catalog. **A.** What happens to his name and address?

_____

_____

B. When will be the _next time_ he hears from you?

_____

_____

5. Based on what I read in this chapter, here are the changes I'll make immediately in how we keep in touch . . .

_____

_____

_____

_____

_____

EPILOGUE

About Your Price

Setting your price for your product or service was once so simple. All you did was add up your costs—labor, materials, salaries, promotional expense, warehousing—and then add one final item to the total—your profit. It baffles many of today's business people that this *cost plus pricing* actually worked.

It succeeded because the American economy was in overdrive. In the 1950s, millions of new households were formed, each requiring a home, furniture, clothing, appliances, and an automobile. Unemployment was low and wages were fair. It was the decade of department stores. Profits were healthy and sustainable.

What a difference a few decades can make. During the 1980s and 90s, most households' buying power declined. In the current U.S. presidential election, one of the candidates reminds voters that the real average hourly wage is 5 percent lower than a decade ago. Today's shopper is paying much closer attention to the price tag. Each major purchase holds an opportunity cost: If I make this purchase, I will have to forego that other product or service I was considering.

Many of today's shrewd marketers have adapted by turning cost plus pricing on its head. They let the customer name the price and then figure out how to make the product profitably at that price. This method is known as *target pricing*. Here are two examples of companies that successfully let their customers help set the price.

A MUSTANG WITH MARKETING MUSCLE

During the early 1960s, General Motors was offering sports car enthusiasts the Corvette. It was fast, sleek, and because it was a subject of traditional cost plus pricing, pricey. Ford Motor Company wanted to compete in the sports car arena and turned to marketer Lee Iacocca for ideas. Iacocca and his staff discovered that growing numbers of people wanted a sports car, but couldn't afford an automobile in the Corvette price range. After extensive consumer research, they decided that $2,500 was the most these budget-conscious enthusiasts would pay.

The new model, the Mustang, would have to do without the costly engine, drive train, and suspension found in a Corvette because such items would pull it out of its target price. But the Mustang sports car had nice styling and bucket seats, and it was affordable. In April 1964, Ford introduced the Mustang with a base price inside the target— $2,368. Ford sold more Mustangs in its first year than any car they had ever built.

LOWERING PRICES THE *RIGHT* WAY

Compaq Computer Company provides another example. Eckhard Pfieffer, CEO, believes that success in today's personal computer industry depends as much on marketing as it does technology. Compaq built its early reputation with high-quality computers and accessories and priced them accordingly. Budget-minded competitors began building the computer equivalent of a Ford Mustang. Most customers couldn't justify paying Corvette-like prices when a

Mustang would get the job done. The consumer was naming his price. Compaq's market share began to erode.

On June 15, 1992, Compaq responded. It announced 45 new models and across-the-board price cuts of up to 32 percent. How could Compaq afford to take the knife to its markup?

- For the first time, Compaq insisted on aggressive competitive bidding from its suppliers. Competitive bidding alone saved $165 million through the third quarter of 1992.

- Factories in Houston, Singapore, and Scotland began running additional shifts, producing twice as many PCs in the same space. In one year, unit costs dropped 52 percent.

- The number of redesigns of process boards for each model was reduced from 14 to 3. The average cost of the boards dropped from $450 to $200 each.

- Testing time for the units, known as "burn-in," was cut from 96 hours to 2. This reduced needed warehouse space by 270,000 square feet.

For Compaq, lowering prices was a marketplace necessity. It might not be for your company. You should think long and hard before following Compaq's lead.

- Are you facing similar pricing pressures?

- Will your customers continue to pay more for your product or service if it performs better than the rest?

CAUTION—FALLING PROFITS

Without careful preparation and fiscal discipline, price cutting sends you into treacherous territory. When you cut your price:

- Your customer concludes that your product was overpriced to begin with.

- You reduce your profit margin. Unless the price cut is accompanied by reduced manufacturing and labor costs, as was the case at Compaq, you'll need a substantial increase in sales volume to remain profitable. Michael V. Marn at McKinsey & Co. points out that a 1 percent drop in price will slash operating profits by 12.3 percent for the average Standard & Poor's 1000 company. His estimate assumes that costs and volume remain the same.
- You create more sales, but you attract the James Tyrones and the "spinners" discussed under the Third Universal Law—Qualify Your Customers. These are the price shoppers who previously bought from a cheaper competitor.
- You achieve only a temporary competitive advantage. If your new price draws customers away from your competitors, your competitors respond with their own price cut.

It's better to set a sustainable price before entering the fray than to succumb to price cuts once you're in the middle of the marketing jungle. The price you create for your product or service must be justifiable. Put it to the test. Create a list of benefits for your product that make it worth the price you've determined. Restrict the list to benefits; do not include features: Features don't justify your price, benefits do. Here are some examples:

Glide™ dental floss is worth twice as much as conventional nylon flosses because:

1. It moves more smoothly between teeth and gums, making it easier to use. The product is particularly beneficial to the less-than-dutiful flosser. There's minimal irritation when passing it through slightly swollen gum tissue.
2. Unlike its lower-priced competition, it won't shred and get stuck between teeth and gums.

Glide is *not* worth twice as much to *all* customers. Some lower priced flosses will generate more sales volume. But sharp retailers know that unit sales aren't as important as the net profit per unit.

Likewise, a meal at a Houston's restaurant is about 10 percent more expensive than a competitive eatery one hundred yards down the road because:

1. Houston's invests more to create a relaxing and attractive atmosphere. It's a more comfortable place to share a meal.

2. Houston's always serves an excellent meal. The cook is trained to inspect her work before presenting the meal for wait staff pick-up. The waiter gives the dish a second going-over. If it's not right, it's not served. And if, after passing the double inspection, you're not satisfied, they'll make it right. (Consistency beats occasional excellence, but *consistent* excellence beats occasional excellence *and* justifies a premium price.)

As previously mentioned, Learningsmith sells educational software at the full suggested retail price. The store on the other side of the mall sells it for 10 percent less. Learningsmith customers are willing to pay more because:

1. Learningsmith is choosey. The store evaluates the quality of the software before deciding to place it on the shelves. (They narrow their offerings). The customer buys with greater confidence.

2. The customer can sit down at a computer inside the store and *try* the new software before deciding to buy. (Risk is removed, and a more intelligent purchase decision is made).

Do you notice how the Universal Laws help justify and maintain profitable pricing? If you're not defying comparison, removing the risk, narrowing your offerings, and delivering consistently, you probably are overpriced.

But before you reach for the red pen, recall and review the results of cutting your price. What you hope will be a quick solution to your problem might throw you into an intractable predicament.

Review each of the Universal Laws and decide which two or three need the most attention. Maybe you have a great product, have it priced right, but aren't keeping in touch. Perhaps you're defying comparison but delivering only sporadic high-quality service. Maintain a profitable price by committing to greater consistency. *Apply the Law before applying the discount.*

PRICE INTEGRITY

Businesses that practice price integrity establish steady, profitable prices for their products and services. Customers of these companies are willing to pay the going rate because they recognize the value the company is adding. Price integrity creates a fair transaction. Everyone pays the same. This "no haggle" strategy is successfully used at Saturn automobile dealerships. The dealer's best price isn't restricted to the hard-nosed bargainer. The Saturn pricing policy also helps limit the merry-go-round ups and downs of sales events and special promotions.

Circuit City, an electronics superstore chain, has entered the rough and tumble world of selling used cars. Their new dealerships, dubbed Car Max, are smoothing away some of the rough spots of the business. In just four Car Max locations in 1995, the operation did an estimated $288 million in sales. Low prices are not the only reason the outlets are attracting customers. Car Max consumer research discovered:

1. **Buyers want the widest possible selection of automobiles.** Car Max responded by stocking between 500 and 1,200 vehicles per location.
2. **Buyers want a simple purchase process.** Touch-screen computers let customers

electronically search for the vehicle that meets their criteria. One Car Max employee handles the sale and the financing.

3. **Buyers do not want to haggle with the salesperson.** They want the lowest possible price without resorting to bazaar-like negotiations. Car Max posts the price on the vehicle and sticks with it.

Price integrity is destroyed when you begin discounting for no apparent reason. Discounting is not the only way to make your product or service more attractive. There are other ways you can offer a better deal without cutting your price. Here are your options:

Something More

Many producers of tangible items are delivering greater value by maintaining price while delivering additional product. The makers of Neutrogena soap could assign a "new lower price" to each bar on the shelf. Instead, the company occasionally offers a "buy one, get one free" promotion. The customer receives twice as much soap for the same price, while price integrity is maintained. The individual bar of soap is not priced lower but the customer receives an occasional excellent deal.

California Pizza Kitchen recently learned in focus groups that customers define value as larger portions. Co-chairman Larry Flax says, "We're learning that people want more for their dollar. It isn't about lowering prices."

McDonald's success was rooted in the good deal. Its growth in the 1960s was fueled by 15-cent hamburgers and 19-cent cheeseburgers. By the 1980s, the expense of surging growth had a steeper price. In 1986, the average cost of opening a new McDonald's was $1.21 million. By 1990, the cost had exploded 28 percent to $1.55 million. Prices for menu items had crept up to keep up, leaving a wide opening for thriftier competitors, like Pepsico's® Taco Bell™.

During the late 1980s, the annual number of transactions per U.S. McDonald's restaurant was declining. Strong international growth made it tempting to avoid addressing the domestic dilemma. The company's approach to the problem focused on cost-cutting and creative pricing. McDonald's adopted a three-pronged approach to better pricing:

1. Everyday low pricing. Hamburgers at 59 cents, cheeseburgers at 69 cents, and $1.99 hamburger Happy Meals™—these prices were an actual reduction from previously posted prices. But notice that McDonald's wasn't running a limited time only sale on hamburgers or cheeseburgers. This was seven-day-a-week pricing. And they didn't adjust prices until they had made a commensurate reduction in their cost structure.

2. Extra Value Meals®. Call it combination pricing. Each combination consisted of a sandwich, a large order of french fries, and a large soft drink for a price lower than the sum of the individually priced items. The customer receives a volume discount. McDonald's only additional cost in the transaction is to pay the *incremental cost* of larger portions, a cost very low in proportion to the retail prices. Remember, before the introduction of Extra Value Meals:

- The labor was behind the counter (and grill).
- The lights were on.
- The soft drink was being poured.

The only changes are the size of the cup for the drink, the larger bag for the fries, and the cost of the additional product.

3. Super-sizing®. An extension of the bigger-size concept. Scooping up a super large box of fries costs McDonald's very little more than delivering a large box of fries. Upping the size of drink and fries currently costs customers 39 cents at most McDonald's outlets.

McDonald's return to value pricing has reversed a late 1980s' trend of customer defections and slower per-unit revenue growth.

Consider the example presented in this book's introduction. Boboli®, the pizza shell makers, announced a "new lower price." Once their price is lowered, it's difficult to return to the original, more profitable price. Boboli could have offered more Boboli for the same price. The television commercial could have shown the product in all of its mouthwatering goodness and *added value* by announcing, "Free pizza-for-one shell in specially marked packages." The existing price is successfully maintained and the customer walks out of the supermarket with more for his money.

Something for Something

If you practice The 7 Universal Laws, you create demand for your product or service. When some or all of the Universal Laws are neglected, demand declines. When demand declines, the price tags get marked down.

There are circumstances when lowering your price is justified and warranted, even in a period of strong sales. Smart discounting creates a win/win. In each of the cases listed below, there's a reason for the discount:

1. **Your customer is buying in large volume.** If a 5 to 10 percent price reduction will produce twice the sales, offer the reduction. Like McDonald's, your incremental cost of making a larger sale might be low. Price integrity is maintained because the discount applies only to those purchasing in large quantity.

2. **You get paid more quickly.** We offer a discount to those clients willing to pay us on the day of our seminar or consulting presentations. It saves the client money (win for them) and saves us from generating an additional invoice as well as improving our cash flow (win for us).

3. **You've reduced your cost of doing business.** Passing savings to customers makes good business

sense. It should increase sales and put pressure on your competitors. Be sure you can live comfortably with the lower price.

SUMMING IT UP

In *The 7 Universal Laws of Customer Value,* I've attempted to help you see your business as an apothecary's scale. One side of the scale is price, the other side, quality. To maintain your profits in a fast-changing market, you have two options. You can subtract from the price side and, unless you've reduced your costs, make a corresponding withdrawal from the quality side of your scale. This book urges you to choose your second option: Add to the quality side, and maintain your balance with a profitable price. Everybody wins when you focus on contributing value.

Treat your customers fairly. Everyone buying the same product in the same quantity should pay the same price. Lower your price only if it benefits you *and* your customers. Enduring businesses create customer relationships for the long haul. Their success is shared with those who purchase their products and services. Pricing decisions should be an integral part of the relationship you create.

If integrity and quality are the words that guide your enterprise, you can't help but succeed.

ENDNOTES

FIRST UNIVERSAL LAW—DEFY COMPARISON

"The Shooting War in Software." *Business Week,* November 8, 1993.

"From the Microbrewers Who Brought You Bud, Coors . . ." *Business Week,* April 24, 1995.

Midwest Express Magazine, May–June 1994.

"Plane Fare." *The Kansas City Star,* July 23, 1995.

"Right Stuff." *Milwaukee Journal Sentinel,* June 26, 1995.

Information Resources Inc. InfoScan Sequential Report, IRI Scan Data for thirteen weeks ending June 18, 1995.

"Stuck - How Companies Cope When They Can't Raise Prices." *Business Week,* December 12, 1993.

"Oprah: The Year of Living Dangerously." *Working Woman,* May 1994.

Godek, Gregory J. P., *1001 Ways To Be Romantic.* Godek has been a guest on Donahue, Oprah and Jenny Jones and felt Oprah was the talk show host best prepared to discuss specific sections of his book.

Phil Kloer. "Oprah Questions Her Genre's Validity." *Atlanta Journal,* September 8, 1994.

"Television Talk Shows Battle it Out for Elusive Ratings." *Los Angeles Times,* November 14, 1994.

"It's My Favorite Statistic." *Forbes,* September 12, 1994.

Eric Kraus, The Gillette Company. Telephone interview, August 15, 1995.

SECOND UNIVERSAL LAW—REMOVE THE RISK

"Try Out Marketing Gains Ground." *New York Times,* January 23, 1995.

Rick Vancisin, Gorton's of Gloucester. Telephone interview, February 13, 1995.

Leticia Fleischer, Learningsmith. Telephone interview, January 10, 1996.

"Mr. Smith Goes to Cyberspace." *Business Week,* October 30, 1995.

Jim Olsen, Northword Press. Telephone interview, February 27, 1995.

"How to Make it Pay." *Business Week,* August 8, 1994.

"It's an Ill Wind." *Forbes,* December 7, 1992.

"Voices of Experience." Recorded April, 1987. National Speakers Association. Audiotape.

"The Business of Teaching." *Los Angeles Times,* November 28, 1991.

"Dating Is a Jungle, so Be a Guerilla." *Atlanta Journal,* January 14, 1993.

"Should You Use a Guarantee to Increase Your Sales?" *Profit-Building Strategies for Business Owners,* December, 1989.

Greg Martin, Saturn Corporation. Telephone interview, February 27, 1995.

"JWT Pledges 15% Spot-Buy Savings." *Advertising Age,* July 19, 1993.

THIRD UNIVERSAL LAW—QUALIFY YOUR CUSTOMERS

O'Neil, Eugene, *Long Day's Journey Into Night* (Yale University Press, 1955).

Winninger, Thomas J., *Price Wars: How to Win the Battle for Your Customer* (St. Thomas Press, 1994).

"Long-distance callers cash in on incentives." *USA Today,* July, 27, 1995.

Reichheld, Frederick F., and W. Earl Sasser, Jr. "Zero Defections: Quality Comes to Services." *Harvard Business Review,* September–October, 1990.

Schrage, Michael, "Fire Your Customers!" *Wall Street Journal,* March 16, 1992.

Brian Adamik, Yankee Group. Telephone interview, October 13, 1995.

Orr, Alicia, "Customers for Life." *Target Marketing,* March, 1995.

John Skalko, AT&T. Telephone interview, October 10, 1995.

Mike Hurd, Saturn Corporation. Telephone interview, October 4, 1995.

Bob Pierce, Pierce Furniture. Telephone interview, October 4, 1995.

Marketing Services Associates. Portland, ME. October, 1993, for *Down East Magazine.*

Hallmark Cards Inc. Used with permission.

Robert Graffy, "Cookin'." Telephone interview, October 4, 1995.

Robert Pompei, Action Automation and Controls. Telephone interview, October 4, 1995.

Frederick F. Reichheld. "Loyalty based Management." *Harvard Business Review,* March–April, 1993.

FOURTH UNIVERSAL LAW—NARROW YOUR OFFERINGS

Alliance Systems. Used with permission.

Jane Brody. Redelmeier is quoted in Brody's Personal Health column. *New York Times,* February 1, 1995.

"Shoppers Easily Influenced Choices." *New York Times,* November 9, 1994.

Pine, B. Joseph II, Bart Victor, and Andrew C. Boynton. "Making Mass Customization Work," *Harvard Business Review.* September–October, 1993.

FIFTH UNIVERSAL LAW—TELL THE TRUTH

Rothenberg, Randall, *Where the Suckers Moon* (Knopf, 1994).

Benn, Alec, *The 27 Most Common Mistakes in Advertising* (Amacom, 1978).

Fry, Robin, *The VW Beetle* (David & Charles Publishing, 1980).

"Heineken's Battle to Stay Top Bottle." *Business Week,* August 1, 1994.

Audiocasette of radio spot provided by Warwick Baker & Fiore.

Joyce DiBona, DiBona, Bornstein & Random. Telephone interview, February 2, 1995.

Kragen, Ken, *Life is a Contact Sport* (Morrow, 1994.)

Charles Horne, Amica Mutual Insurance Company. Telephone interview, February 2, 1995.

"Quicknews: A Newsletter for Intuit Customers," Spring, 1994.

Suzanne Taylor, Intuit. Telephone interview, February 6, 1995.

SIXTH UNIVERSAL LAW—CONSISTENCY BEATS OCCASIONAL EXCELLENCE

John Landers, Red Roof Inn. Telephone interview, November 17, 1995.

Love, John F., *McDonald's Behind the Arches Revised Edition* (Bantam Books, 1995). I could write another book about Ray Kroc and McDonald's. Before I get carried away, let me recommend Love's book and *Grinding it Out* by Ray Kroc (St. Martin's Press. 1992).

Nancy Lawrence, Portmanteau. Personal interview, November 22, 1995.

Christine McPartland, Marcam Corporation. Telephone interview, November 20, 1995.

Scott Faulds, Intuit. Telephone interview, December 1, 1995.

SEVENTH UNIVERSAL LAW—KEEP IN TOUCH (MORE THAN A BILL)

Nancy Lawrence, Portmanteau. Personal interview, November 22, 1995.

Grassfield, Max, "The Personal Touch." *Target Marketing,* March, 1995.

Viking Office Products. Used with permission.

EPILOGUE—ABOUT YOUR PRICE

Nagle, Thomas T., and Reed K. Holden. *The Strategy and Tactics of Pricing—A Guide to Profitable Decision Making* (Prentice Hall. 1995).

"The Revolution at Compaq." *Fortune,* December 24, 1992.

"Stuck!—How Companies Cope When They Can't Raise Prices." *Business Week,* November 15, 1993.

Circuit City spokesperson. Telephone interview. January 4, 1995.

"Beyond Quality and Value." *Fortune,* special issue, Autumn/Winter 1993.

Love, John F., *McDonald's—Behind the Arches—Revised Edition.* Bantam Books. 1995.

I am grateful to my professional speaking colleague, Jim Hennig, PhD, CPAE, who introduced me to the concepts of price integrity and "something for something."

INDEX

ABOUT THE AUTHOR

Steve Broydrick is president of Steve Broydrick Associates, a customer service training and marketing consulting firm, based in Portland, Maine.

Steve's seminars and training programs are thoroughly customized, through on site visits and telephone interviews with current customers, lapsed customers, and employees. Over the years, this observation work has contributed to a vast body of knowledge about customer value and customer expectations—and is the impetus for this book.

Among Steve's clients are North Shore Medical Center (Salem, MA), Providence Medical Center (Kansas City, KS), Pennsylvania Cable Television Association, Frederick News-Post (MD), Johnson & Dix Oil Co. (Lebanon, NH).

Steve is a graduate of Williams College in Massachusetts.